The best kind of book for personal growth is one that has deep truths that are written in practical ways so you can implement them into your daily life. That is exactly what you'll find in Dangerous Prayers. Get ready to pray some Dangerous Prayers!

~Randy Bezet, Lead Pastor of Bayside Community Church

Dangerous Prayers is like having Spiritual cataract surgery. Everything is clearer now. I have been praying much more and worrying less and started to experience more answered prayer in the last two weeks. The stories are captivating, making the book difficult to put down. This book will inspire you to believe bigger and more specifically for the God-sized dreams in your heart. I believe this is a 'must-read' for anyone who desires to walk more fully in the favor and power of Jesus Christ.

~Ben Rodgers, Executive Director Children's Cup

From the first look, I knew Dangerous Prayers was God-breathed. The lessons Pastor Alex wants us all to learn are so simple, yet so profound. This book can change your life, if you will let it.

~Kelly Stilwell, Professional Blogger at Virtually Yours

Dangerous Prayers is captivating like a bedtime story from God the Father Himself. My take is that it needs to be required reading for humans (period). Sums up who we are and the power we have in the Kingdom. Thank you for getting it in my hands. It's going to be big!

~Dr.Guy S. DaSilva, M.D.

Alex has always been a dear friend to me and Dangerous Prayers is a life-giving, Biblical approach to changing your life one prayer at a time. This will be a book you'll want to read over and over again because you will experience encouragement and I believe life change each and every time.

~Jordan Becnel, Worship Pastor at Bayside Community Church

Dangerous Prayers is an encouraging and inspiring blend of great story telling and Biblical truths. Pastor Alex Anderson has written a great book for anyone going through the storms of life or who desires growth in their personal prayer time. I was drawn in as much by the real life struggles and heartaches of people as by the power of prayer.

~Jared Florian, Chairman and CEO of Screen Arts

Alex is an expert at making the power of God's Word and promises practical and alive. I learned in Dangerous Prayers to ask God to fill my mind with His perfect plans for my life and then stand in agreement with Him to empower those dreams. The conversational style of this book really draws the reader in. It's as if I were sitting down having a conversation with Alex and him teaching me how to connect with God's immeasurable power.

~Randy Wadle, CEO of NetWise Technology

Alex Anderson demonstrates how Dangerous Prayers will unleash God's power and be answered. Written in a casual, easy-to-read style illustrated with personal examples of friends encountering major problems in life who prayed dangerously, it shows how God responded. This book was an eye-opener, making me think about the clarity and laser-like focus of prayer, thereby changing my way of praying. It's a "page turner" must read for believers.

~Roger P. Conley, P.A.

After reading Dangerous Prayers, your mountains won't seem so impossible to move! Pray those BOLD prayers and change your life as well as others. I never knew a book could be so funny and life changing all at the same time.

~LaRinda Massey

Dangerous Prayers is a page-turner to be read deliberately. The author's sense of humor and relaxed style, combined with his deep understanding and presentation of Scriptures causes misty eyes and Holy Ghost bumps in many episodes. We can see that God is moved by a passionate desire of deliberate prayers, such as needs and thoughts made verbal when your heart speaks. It is an in-depth message about prayer that needs repeating and therefore a book that can be read repeatedly for knowledge and inspiration.

~Dr. and Mrs. Frederick J. Witt

If you really want to know how to live a life blessed with answered prayers, Dangerous Prayers is filled with the keys you have been searching for. Alex opens the eyes of believers by showing us how prayer is supposed to work for healing and changed lives. Through story after story Alex illustrates exactly how to live a life blessed with answered prayers by digging deep into our faith, trusting God with a vision for our future, and listening intently to what He has to say about our lives. I dare you to read this book!

~Amy Gaston, Educator

Through Dangerous Prayers, Pastor Alex will take you from When-I-wish-upon-a-star weak and lifeless prayers to dynamic, life-changing prayers that will not only impact you but the world around you.

~Robin Hatch

Pastor Alex, through his teachings, has completely changed our family's life. Had it not been for his mentoring us about having true, dangerous prayers, I honestly believe we would not be living in our dream house today. Once you truly grasp the concept of praying Dangerous Prayers, you will never look at life the same again. You are FOREVER changed.

~Leanne Parsons Baker

I would highly recommend reading Dangerous Prayers if you are ready to increase your faith. Thank you for writing a book that is critical for a Christian's spiritual life. Dangerous Prayers teaches us how instrumental our prayers are to ignite God's supernatural power over our lives. If you will start a habit of praying dangerously, your life will never be the same. Thank you for impacting mine.

~Stacy Goodwin

Pastor Alex teaches the need to be specific, to believe, and most importantly to talk to God like you already have it. I took the initiative and did just that. And it forever changed the way I pray. I am forever thankful for this man's wisdom. I am a living testimony of the value of Dangerous Prayers.

~Jarod Gordon, Men's Director of 24/7 School of Ministry.

To my wife, my companion, encourager, helpmate, co-heir and best friend. You have always been my biggest cheerleader and have supported me all these crazy years. I love you and without your Dangerous Prayers for me, I would not even be around to write this book. I love you babe! And thank you!

DANGEROUS

PRAYERS

YOU WILL NEVER LOOK AT PRAYER THE SAME

Contents

ISBN: 978-0-9913634-0-7

INTRODUCTION
A Warning about Dangerous Prayers!

Dear Reader,

A part of me hopes that you don't have to read this book.

In fact, there's nothing I'd like more for you than for your life situation to be exactly how you want it to be right now. Maybe you have plenty of money. You are enjoying excellent health. You're engaged in fulfilling relationships. And you're living your God-inspired passion and purpose for your life. However, there's a pretty good chance you aren't there yet, and no matter how hard you've tried, you can't seem to get there. It might just be time for a Dangerous Prayer.

So a quick opening thought on what Dangerous Prayers aren't.

Dangerous Prayers are not magic bullets or one- size-fits-all quick fixes.

Not to discourage you by any means, but it will take a lot of motivation to pray Dangerous Prayers. They aren't the safe little blurbs you fire off to heaven right before you play the lottery. Nor are these the "fake a headache" prayers you sheepishly knock out before eating in public. Nope.

These prayers take courage and will cost you something before they get answered. It could be sleep, time, money, reputation, pride or even going against tradition or empirical data. I don't really know what the price will be for you, but I do know that if you have a big enough *why* then it will be worth it.

What exactly is a Dangerous Prayer?

Let me bring you up to speed on a very important piece of knowledge you need before you tear off into the wild blue yonder praying dangerously. It's about the term Dangerous Prayer. You need to know how it came about and why I use it.

In the earlier stages of writing this book, my friend Mike was editing some of the draft chapters and after he finished he said, "You know P.A. (an aka for Pastor Alex), this is not your ordinary book on prayer. The people in this book actually get their prayers answered and some of them dangerously. Why don't you consider calling it something like *Dangerous Prayers*?"

I chewed it over for a bit and realized he was right. At first I just wanted to encourage you to pray with the hope that you would have better results after reading the real-life stories of my friends practicing the Dangerous Prayer principles in this book. With thirty years of amazing anecdotes to choose from, it was a slam-dunk, pick-me-up kind of book.

But when Mike said, "These are Dangerous Prayers," I had to agree. Not just because some of them are spectacular and they all actually get answered, but also because they are, in a biblical sense, prayers. And despite the possibility of getting answers you don't expect or want, there are principles behind these prayers that cause them to work. These aren't magic formulas. Anyone can learn them, which means that you can too!

Some Bible Stuff about Dangerous Praying

In the book of Matthew, we read some very strange words that rolled off the lips of our Lord Jesus Christ.

"From the days of John the Baptist until now, the kingdom of heaven suffers violence, and violent men take it by force." Matthew 11:12 NAS

At first glance this verse has some pretty bizarre wording, like the *kingdom of heaven suffers violence* and violent *men take it by force.* And like most things at first glance, it is not as it appears. It reads like something from a Star Wars episode where powerful hooded forces of light and darkness are clutching each other's throats and the hero of the light is losing to the dark side. Unfortunately it's not as theatrical as what happens in the movies, or we might just pay more attention.

Something very dynamic and powerful, however, was taking place in such a noticeable way that the Lord Jesus felt it necessary to mention it. And Matthew thought it of enough interest to write it in his Gospel. After all, Matthew did not write down everything Jesus did or said, only those things Holy Spirit decided we should know about some 2000 thousand years later.

So what are these invisible (or not so invisible) forces and struggles that have and continue to take place? And what do they have to do with our prayers?

Cousin John

John the Baptist, Jesus' wild-eyed, locust-and-honey-eating recluse of a cousin, was the first to start talking (loudly) of the strange goings on. As a prophet, John had his pick of the litter when it came to topic matter, but for some reason he zoned in on the Kingdom of Heaven. He told them that something big was coming and wanted to make sure that no one missed out on it. And despite John's throwback camel hair suit and strange ways, everyone wanted in. He drew quite a crowd.

Being the simple guy John was, he had a straightforward, two-step plan to close the deal. Step one: Repent. This meant to change the way you think about God and act toward others—to change your heart. Being nice wasn't good enough. No, John was all about putting it all on the line for God or not at all.

And his step two was as tough as step one. No putting your toe in the water for him, no sir. You had to show everyone you meant business, that you were the real deal. So bring an extra change of clothes because it was all about full immersion. Step two: Baptism.

He took you all the way under. Funny, I don't think John the Sprinkler or John the Splasher would have had as much staying power.

Anyway John's message started a tidal wave that helped kick off his cousin Jesus' ministry. Most don't know that John was simply getting everyone warmed up for Jesus and many of the Lord's original disciples came from John's wild-eyed ways. People were making real commitments and taking serious action to get ready for the Kingdom of Heaven. The sheer volume of people coming by the droves to John to be baptized and the pushy and radical lifestyle changes people were making from their hearts prompted the Lord Jesus to make this comment that Matthew wrote in his gospel: *"...violent men take it by force."*

Dangerous Decisions

Those who were pushing and forcing their lives to now line up with John's rules for entering the Kingdom of Heaven became marked men and women. By joining John's club, they were risking their lives. They were getting ready for the biggest thing to ever happen to planet earth. Little did these radicals know that their King would be arriving sooner than they thought.

No questions about it, it was a grand start, but in order to make radical and permanent lifestyle changes, something deeper had to happen in John's disciples. Their very nature had to be replaced. The very seat of their being had to be ripped out and a new one installed. I'm talking about man's spirit, not his mind, will, emotions or his body. When the very core of a person's nature is replaced, then over time, the rest of their humanity will follow. And the rules of how that happens changed dramatically once Jesus came, died, rose again, and took off for Heaven, leaving us the Holy Spirit.

Cousin John didn't fully get the mechanics of all that would eventually happen through Jesus. The best John could do was get the crowd revved up and ready to go. But John showed what people who were violent and dangerous could do. Violent and dangerous actions cause things to happen. These people were taking a personal risk by following John's advice and signing up to be a part of this new kingdom. The Jewish leaders of his day didn't take it very kindly when a new club was growing at the expense of their membership. For a few crazies to leave the temple probably was a good thing. They were trying to figure out what to do with that riff-raff anyhow. When the good ones—the paying customers—starting disappearing, well now, that had to stop. So cousin John eventually lost his head over it.

The fact remained that most of John's violent followers became the followers of Jesus and those who hung around long enough, at least until Peter preached his first message, became Dangerous. Not only to the Jewish leadership of the day, but to the god of this world, Satan. Satan began to lose his grip on multitudes as Christ's followers began to realize the power they had been entrusted with as a result of their subsequent empowerment by Holy Spirit.

Holy Spirit gets a New Job

Jesus sent Him from heaven with a different ministry than He had ever had on earth. His new job description was to take ordinary cowards like Peter, you and me and then turn us into Dangerous weapons against the god of this world. 1 John 3:8 states that, *"Jesus came to destroy the works of the devil."* Jesus was Dangerous to the kingdom of Satan. Satan's club membership numbers were taking a beating.

And "was" is correct, because Jesus is not here on earth. We are. We are to continue his work. The Dangerous work of destroying the works of the Devil isn't up to the angels or saints; it's our job. Don't believe me? Then check this out:

"Very truly I tell you, whoever believes in me will do the works I have been doing, and they will do even greater

7

things than these, because I am going to the Father." John 14:12 NIV

Yep you read it right, that means you and me, boss. We got the right stuff to do the work and the number one way we release the stuff is through prayer. Say it with me. We release the stuff through prayer. One more time, please! We release the stuff through prayer. Good job!

Nothing happens on earth for the kingdom until someone releases the stuff (my word for the will and power of God). We are God's agents and we are to be Dangerous in our praying. We spread the life of the kingdom of heaven, the life Jesus died for all to live, through Dangerous Prayer. Dangerous Praying is the most powerful and effective way to spread the kingdom around and destroy the works of the devil. Check out this verse from James:

"...pray for each other so that you may be healed. The prayer of a righteous person is powerful and effective." James 5:16 NIV

So Dangerous Prayer is where it starts. It lights the fuse to the stick of dynamite that causes an avalanche of damage to the other guy's kingdom, the god of this world.

Real People, Real Prayers, Real Answers

In the following pages, you will read the stories of real people with real life problems who prayed real Dangerous

Prayers that ripped their situations out of the hands of their enemy and put them in a position of strength. Like when Mad Mack prayed dangerously for his son who hated him after a nasty divorce only to see their relationship restored.

Or like when Lori dangerously prayed forgiveness over those who did not deserve it and was healed from thirteen years of diseases.

Maybe your business is dying or almost dead, and like Ryan, you need to pray a Dangerous Prayer and see it resurrected back to life.

You may have just gotten some gut-wrenching news about a loved one and need to pray dangerously like John did and be the one God uses to bring healing to everyone wiped out by the emotional tsunami.

Hopefully you haven't been sued lately, but if you have, Gary's Dangerous Prayer may help you with your lawsuit. Well, at least up to the size of his—$2.5 million. After that you'll have to write your own Dangerous Prayer.

I don't know what you are facing right now, but I know this: if you are dealing with sucker punches from the god of this world, you need to start praying dangerously. And I am hopeful these words are exactly what you need to be reading for such a time as this. Life happens whether we pray or not. Please don't be unprepared, because you don't have to be.

And hey, read this book with a prayer partner. It will enhance your experience. I also recommend you join our Dangerous Prayer Community. Find us on Facebook and Dangerous-Prayers.com. Stay connected, start praying dangerously, and I look forward to seeing and hearing about the amazing things God can do!

THIS BOOK BELONGS TO:

_____

MY PRAYER PARTNER IS:

_____

TODAY'S DATE IS:

_____

PRAYER ONE
God Always Answers My Prayers

There is no mystery. You can know without a doubt that God will answer your prayers.

Cast Members

My wife and I planned our first Disney World family vacation like most, on paper. Everything looks good on paper right? We had checklists, maps, even an itinerary of the rides we were going to enjoy. We had never been to Disney World with our children and we were all very excited. We planned everything right down to the amount of hand sanitizer needed for all the restroom and restaurant visits. What we did not plan very well was the week we were going.

Okay, so maybe it was obvious to many, but somehow we didn't connect the dots that during the week of Christmas, half of all of humanity would decide to attend the park as well. They must have gotten the same Mouse House mind control signal we got from the Disney satellite in the stratosphere while we were sleeping.

Come to Disney World during the week of Christmas. Miss the crowds who stay home celebrating the holiday.

It was elbow room only. And as luck would have it, our youngest daughter began to run a low-grade fever while we were there, so I rented a stroller for her to ride in. Not only were there long lines everywhere, but also we now had a steamroller to help channel our frustration—I mean, maneuver. Throw in a wave of low pressure that settled in and dumped blinding rain on us the whole week we were there, and you had the perfect family getaway. It was a miserable and unexpected situation for all five of us.

But something shocked us and turned it around. Not only did our uncomfortable situation become much more tolerable, it became fun, thanks to our interaction with the Disney employees. Allow me to explain.

I had finally made it to the front of the line to buy food for my small tribe, praying I had remembered all the various dietary details of their requests correctly so I would not have to re-enter the line that seemed to now encircle metro Orlando. I was ready, with my wife's help, to communicate the order to the cashier. As I turned to her, she smiled the brightest smile, and with a very comforting and calming tone said, "How may I serve you, sir?"

In the midst of being wet and tired, her warm sunny smile and tone of voice was so refreshing. It was a game-

14

changer. Her bright and positive demeanor instantly became Disney's "secret weapon" against the crowds and horrible weather.

While the food was being collected and stacked for my clan, I felt myself relaxing enough to create small talk. I noticed that written just below the cashier's name on her nametag was Dayton, Ohio. I asked her why she decided to work so far away from home. Why had she come to Florida? She then said, with the same sunny smile and soothing tone of voice, "Oh, sir, that would be much too boring to discuss. I would much rather hear about your fun here at Disney World." Darn it! She just would not let me stay in my funk.

As soon as she said those words, our food arrived. After I thanked her, she said, "You're most welcome, sir. Glad to be of service."

She magically turned a bad day into fun! My whole Disney experience was for the better as I was constantly greeted with cheerful smiles and courteous responses from this amazing team of people.

Another killer thing I noticed while at Disney World was that on certain doors and gates were signs that were labeled, "Cast Members Only". I understood later that those doors and gates led to secret passageways that employees used to be transported to other places in the park without being noticed, perhaps carrying garbage cans or supplies. This whole amazing experience caused me to be intrigued with what went on behind the scenes at Disney. So, after our vacation I began to do some intentional reading and expert research about Disney, which gave me cause to appreciate the organization even more. I read a lot of information about them, but what blew me away the most was their Cast Member Training.

The training Disney provides to their "cast" is so extensive that they have no quality control department. When the employees step on to their sets at Disney, they also step into character. This is why the fun cashier had a bright and sunny smile on her face. This was who she was. She was in her character. The "My pleasure, sir," is the way that her character would normally act.

Disney has made it smokin' easy to perform these actions by making the actions a part of the DNA of the character the employee is playing. They all acted from the way they saw themselves, or rather, their character. While the cast member was at Disney, their personal identity, to a degree, became the same identity of the character they were playing. This is world class! This was everywhere, in every part of Disney World. Even with the rain, the crowds, and my daughter's mild fever, it made our stay, well, "magical".

Connecting the Dots

"There were certainly many types of thoughts that would have been considered unthinkable to Jesus... If we want to follow in His footsteps, then we must begin to think as He did." ~Joyce Meyer, *Battlefield of the Mind*

Our Disney experience really got me thinking about the power of identity. The way we act on a daily basis and how we act from the way we see ourselves, our identity. The things we do or should be doing automatically because of who and what we are affiliated with. With the cast members at the Magic Kingdom, there was no doubt, no question, and no wavering from the role they played once they stepped foot on the kingdom property.

Shockwaves ran through my mind as I began thinking of a different Kingdom and all of its "cast members". What do they look like to the rest of the world? How do they act? And how should they act? What does an affiliation and identity in Christ really mean? Is there the same consistency and power of belief as those following Mickey Mouse? Then suddenly another shockwave, "What about prayer?"

How was it that certain Christ followers got their prayers answered? I wondered if there were any connections with identity and answered prayer. What separates the spaghetti prayers folks throw at the wall hoping they'll stick from the ones that come from a core belief that God is listening and will actually answer every time? So, I scrutinized the life of someone who got His prayers answered every single time, year after year. Jesus.

As a student of the Bible for over thirty-five years, I don't ever recall a time where Jesus' prayers were not answered. Was this because He was God's Son, or because He saw himself as someone whose prayers were always answered?

Jesus never would have looked at his disciples and said, while praying at Lazarus's tomb, "I don't know about this boys. This is going to be hard. Maybe if I had read a little more of the Law of Moses this morning or if had not lost my temper yesterday and ran those guys out of the temple..."

No way! He would have never thought of anything other than, "Lazarus, come forth." As a matter of fact, He states in the scriptures that the only reason He prayed out loud was to encourage those around Him; Martha, Mary and the rest of Lazarus's family and friends.

Jesus Grew into His Identity

Jesus wasn't born with the same identity in His soul that He had at thirty years old; He grew in favor with God and man. He was so much more than Joseph's son, but that knowledge came with time. He spent time learning about who

He was. He wasn't just Joseph's son. He wasn't just a carpenter.

Remember when Jesus was twelve and His parents went to Jerusalem for the Passover Festival? After the celebrations were over, Mary, Joseph, and the rest of the family started back home. Perhaps because it was a large group of extended family, they didn't notice that Jesus wasn't with them. At the end of their first day's journey, when they did the family head count for dinner, they noticed He was missing. They went back to Jerusalem, and after three days of searching, found Him at the Temple sitting among the religious teachers and asking questions. He was in total submission to the process.

For his age, Jesus was asking monster-sized questions. In fact, the teachers thought His questions were so well thought out that they were shocked as well as marveled. He was aggressively growing into His identity. His parents were amazed when they found Him. His mother asked Him a simple question, "Why have you done this to us? Your father and I have been franticly looking for you everywhere."

It was Jesus' response that helps us understand that He had grown in His identity. "Why did you need to search for me? Did you not know I would be in my Father's house?" What a surreal and revealing comment!

Jesus was not being disrespectful. He was declaring His identity. Jesus' parents knew who He was, His real identity, but they "held these things in their heart". I don't think Mary and Joseph sat down with their son and said, "Now, Jesus, the reason you are doing this is because..." I believe Jesus, just like us, grew into His identity. Yes, He was born to a virgin. Yes, He was born of the Spirit. Yes, He was God's sinless son. But He had a soul (mind, will, and emotions), and that took time to develop, just like ours does. There was nothing abnormally supernatural about this growth into His identity as God's son. He came up through the ranks like we do. He spent time being educated and trained like all Jewish young men. He renewed His mind, just as Romans 12:2 recommends. He studied and memorized scriptures, which gave Him the pictures for His mind to use to erase obstacles that could keep Him from His highest calling. The glaring truth is that *you and I are no different*. There is no secret sauce.

After He had spent some eighteen years (from around twelve years old until He was thirty) growing into His identity, He went to John the Baptist to be baptized. This was when the Holy Spirit descended upon Him like a dove, and His Father in Heaven even gave a shout out.

"You are my dearly loved Son, and you bring me great joy."

God the Father is just that up close and personal with us.

Jesus knew His identity, the Holy Spirit knew His identity, and so did His Father in Heaven, but now it was time for Jesus to let the world know. And in good form, He started at His home church. And like it sometimes happens with those who know you too well, or think they know you, His "debut" was not so well received.

Jesus was at the temple one day, and it was His is turn to read the scrolls. After they were brought to Him, He took His time, carefully rolling them out. He then read a portion of Isaiah. When finished, He handed the scrolls back to the attendant. As all eyes were on Him, He began to speak to them, saying, *"This passage came true today when you heard me read it."* Luke 4:21 GWT

Some liked his little message and some did not. Either way, Jesus had declared to the world whom He was! From that day forward, He never thought of prayers not getting answered. It never even dawned on Him. He knew who He was. His brothers and the townspeople didn't, but the Holy Spirit, Heavenly Father and Jesus did. And that's all that mattered!

"Yeah, but He's Jesus."

You might be saying, "Yeah, but He's Jesus." This is more of an excuse than truth—that is, if we consider the Bible to be truth. We should never hide behind our religion. We should be "dangerous" with our praying like Jesus.

"I tell you the truth, anyone who believes in me will do the same works I have done, and even greater works, because I am going to be with the Father." John 14:12

The Bible says we are to identify ourselves with Christ. Galatians 2:20 states this: *"I have been crucified with Christ and I no longer live, but Christ lives in me."*

We may live in earthy bodies, but we can have the same trust in God to answer our prayers as Jesus did! If we identify ourselves with Christ the way the scripture encourages us to, then we would act like the employees and staff of Disney World as they identify themselves as "cast members". Scripture identifies us in Christ as "Sons and Daughters of God".

So did Jesus expect to get his prayers answered? Of course! As Christ followers, we are His body on earth. So, yes, even to this day, Jesus expects us to get our prayers answered as well. Is that how we are praying? Don't answer that yet!

It should never cross our mind that God would not answer our prayer, just like it never crossed Jesus' mind. It would never occur in the minds of the Disney cast to say anything other than, "How may I serve you?" "Good to see you", or "My pleasure". You would never hear them say, "What do you want?" or bust out laughing uncontrollable and say to us "I don't have time for that," because it's not who they are. They are Disney cast members and that's how they identify themselves. It's what they do because it's who they are. Christ followers expect to get their prayers answered, too, because it's who they are.

Change of Mind

"The only time my prayers are never answered is on the golf course." ~Billy Graham

One of the things a Christ-follower can do to grow into their identity is found in Roman 12:2. We should not copy the behavior of people who do not get their prayers answered. It's a very common thing for people not to get their prayers answered. But it should not be this way for Christ-followers. God is more than willing to answer our prayers, but He will not control our will, so we must first identify ourselves to him as someone who believes that He will answer our prayers.

You see, as Christ-followers, there is nothing, spiritually speaking, that would prevent us from having our prayers answered. It is our soul, the location of our believed identity; how we see ourselves that is the key. Our mind, will, and emotions are the parts of our soul. It is in our soul that we can think like a person who believes *God always answers my prayers*. Then we begin to feel like *God always answers my prayers.* Finally, we jump to the next level and act like *God always answers my prayers.*

So don't copy the ways of those who choose not to identify with Jesus, who say things like, "I don't know if God really answers all prayers. Some prayers he answers, and others he doesn't."

The truth is, God does answer all prayers and you are not off the hook!

Christ-followers know this. They know God. For them to think any other way is to think the way the majority of the world thinks. Those who are not Christ followers do not know Him and do not expect to get their prayers answered.

So how does Jesus think about prayer? Well, it never crosses His mind that God won't answer His prayer. It should be the same for Christ followers. It should never cross your mind, "Will God answer my prayer?" Your only thought should be, "Of course He will."

Christ-followers identify themselves with Christ's death and resurrection and are born-again with recreated spirits. It's this same iron-clad identity that will help you believe *God always answers my prayers.* After our salvation, it is up to us to take responsibility for the care of our souls (mind, will and emotions) with Holy Spirit's help and our continued identity with Christ. Remember, even Jesus himself grew into His identity.

The New You

"I am doing things that are true to me."

~Johnny Depp

What does this mean for you? Consider this: your identity is very critical when it comes to getting your prayers answered. Before you pray, think about who you are. Refuse to pray like those who do not get their prayers answered. Know and believe who you are. Philippians 2:5-8 NLT encourages us with these words:

"You must have the same attitude that Christ had. Even though He was God, He gave up His divine privilege, took the humble position of a slave and was born a human being. When He appeared in human form, He humbled Himself in obedience to God and died a criminal's death."

This is very powerful when it comes to identity. If you are going to humble yourself and do what God wants you to do, then you must change your former identity. It is now out of date. It has expired. It's way behind in technology. It can't even begin to keep up with God's "bandwidth" for His downloads. You must identify with thinking like Christ thinks. Even today, as He sits at the right hand of our Father in Heaven praying for us, He believes *God always answers my prayers.* I don't know what else He would be doing. Maybe making a new solar system?

We always have the option to stay full of our old identity, letting it rule our soul and forfeiting our right to have our prayers answered. Our old identity says, *I don't know if God will answer my prayer.* The old identity likes to live on its own means. It takes a boatload of humility to have the mindset of Christ to believe *God always answers my prayers.* It's so much easier to solve a problem on your own, not to mention more gratifying to the ego or to the old identity; the old unchanged way of thinking.

That's how regular human beings think and act, not like those who get their prayers answered.

It takes a huge, humble heart to say, "How may I serve you?" "Good to see you, sir," or "God always answers my prayers."

The Audacity to Believe It

As a senior associate pastor at Bayside Community, a rapidly- growing church of about 5,000+ members in Bradenton, Florida, I've had the chance to see this paradigm shift play itself out in the lives of many believers. Take, for example, the comments from one of our campus pastors:

"When I grabbed hold of the statement that *God always answers my prayers,* I can say that in the last two years, I have seen God answer more prayers than He has in my entire lifetime. With that one statement and that concept came a new understanding that I never had before. I realized it's not my reputation on the line. It is God's. I was relieved of all the responsibility to make the prayer come to pass. That was up to God. It was because I had the faith and the audacity to believe it that I actually prayed for a couple, and two weeks later God healed the wife of a tumor. Her husband said his wife thinks that I have a direct connection with God. I told him to tell her that I do and you can, too." ~Pastor Mark C.

An Exercise in Identity and Humility

You've seen it on television shows and heard it said, "Now, I have over twenty years of experience. This is not something you should attempt at home." Something like eating fire might not be a good thing to try at home, but believing God always answers your prayers is. The basis for this is found in the following passage of scripture:

"I tell you the truth, anyone who believes in me will do the same works I have done, and even greater works, because I am going to be with the Father." John 14:12 NLT

I honest-to-God don't know how a person could misunderstand this verse. Jesus Christ encouraged His followers to get out there and do what He did. So if you are a Christ-follower, *do* try this at home: For the next week, experiment with a little exercise in identity and humility. Pray Dangerous Prayers!

Say, "God always answers my prayers," out loud to yourself. Try it on for size. See how you like it. Just like your favorite pair of shoes, it might feel a little uncomfortable at first. But I'm betting over time the fit will loosen up. Who knows, you may find yourself saying, "God always answers my prayers," without thinking twice. That's when transformation takes place. Who knows? Life might get real exciting for you as your prayers get answered faster than you even dreamed possible!

Mad Mack

That simple little change may be just what you need to connect with God. It was that way for Mack. Mack was a very successful businessman. He ran a multi-million dollar company that he built from the ground up. Mack could do just about anything he set his mind to. Just about anything. But the one thing Mack could not do was to make his son love him—until he learned to pray dangerously, and that changed everything.

PRAYER TWO
Mad Mack's Prayer

The secret to praying others into the Kingdom without violating their will.

Mad Mack

The first time I met Mad Mack I was somewhat intimidated by him. A manager of a construction firm, he was in charge of a division that built large apartment complexes for developers. I remember him telling me once how tight the profit line had to be in order to be successful when working on such large projects. The daily grind of living on the thin edge of success probably contributed greatly to Mad Mack's demeanor.

He always looked to me like he had either just left a fight, or was getting ready to have one. He was usually red-faced and cursed a lot, sometimes just to himself, but often while talking to others as well. He had a tendency to be very animated and would wave his hands in the air when he was describing a situation. He frequently yelled at people when he talked on the telephone. In his defense, this was due partially to the fact that he had survived significant hearing loss in both ears, but most people didn't know that. They just thought he was mad all the time. I never knew what happened to his hearing. At any rate, my tenure of knowing and interacting with Mad Mack lasted about a year.

This Is Going To Be Painful

Some years after meeting Mad Mack, my wife and I began to attend a new church in a nearby town. We had been there for over a year when I met and became friends with Ted, a local businessman. I invited Ted to come to our church, and after a while he became somewhat of an evangelist, frequently bringing people with him. He and his wife, Julia, loved the church and began to invite everyone they met.

One Sunday morning, my wife and I were greeting at the front door of our church. Ted and Julia came walking across the parking lot with another couple I did not recognize. This wasn't unusual considering the number of new people Ted had been dragging kicking and screaming to church with him who now loved it. When they arrived at the front door, I quickly recognized the man. It was Mad Mack. I honestly thought to myself, *This is going to be painful.*

To be perfectly honest, I was not very excited about seeing Mack, especially at my church home. As he, Ted, and their wives approached the front door, I spent more than the usual amount of time with the couple that were a few feet ahead of them. I had my back towards Ted and Mack. Ted reached over and tapped me on the shoulder and, as I turned around, my eyes met Mad Mack's. I was totally shocked at what I saw. His crystal blue eyes were full of sweet compassion. I could instantly tell that Mad Mack was a different man. He didn't look mad anymore, and I would later repent of my attitude.

Mack and Bonnie, like Ted and Julia, became very committed to the Lord. Like Ted, Mack became an evangelist for our church too. Over the days and weeks, Mack and I began to hang out for lunch. I found out that as a child he had actually given his heart to Jesus, but in his teen years, like many others, he had left the church and God. Mack said he had a nasty dysfunctional relationship with his father, which left him thinking that his Heavenly Father must be nasty as well. For over thirty years, he joined the ranks of those attending church on Christmas and Easter only.

I Just Left Him Alone

Mack had left the firm where we first met and had built a very successful business of his own with annual revenues in excess of $22 million a year. He had gone through a horrible divorce that had in his words, "stripped him" of his self worth. It was after the crushing blow of his divorce that he began to

31

search for the God of his childhood. He said he had "nothing to lose in trying God out again". God answered his prayer, and his heart could again sense that same love and peace he remembered from decades ago.

Shortly after getting back up close and personal with Jesus Christ, tremendous blessings began to take place in Mack's life. He met Bonnie, who was a Christ-follower, and they were married a year and half later. Her encouragement helped him leave the previous firm and start his own, which was off the chain successful.

As I listened to Mack's amazing story, I was squirming in my seat with mixed emotions. One was that I was ashamed of my actions. I was a Christ-follower when I first met Mack but was so distracted by his Mad Mack ways that he probably didn't even know I was a believer. I was not intentionally rude or unkind to him; I just left him alone. I think I was just being a coward. The other emotion was gratefulness, even though back then I didn't want to have anything to do with Mad Mack, God did. Jesus was with him the whole time, waiting patiently for Mad Mack to come to Him. Jesus wanted to answer his prayer long before Mad Mack even knew to ask.

It was then that I repented of my attitude. I prayed, "God help me to stop judging others just because I don't like how they act." God taught me that only He could see into other people's hearts. I could not. I wasn't able to see what nightmarish past events caused people to act the way they do. My job is just to love them, unconditionally. Even to this day, I have this bulldog awareness inside of me that pulls on my heart when I am hurt by others and want to judge their actions. Not always at first, but eventually, over time, I give in to God and am totally free of the event. It's a wonderful gift from God.

The Son of Mad Mack

Most of Mack's life was very blessed. He learned to surrender one part of his life at a time to God. As he continued to ask for God's blessings, he became more and more blessed. However, one part of Mack's life was not as he or God wanted it.

Mack had a son from his previous marriage that lived with he and Bonnie. Phillip did not like his father. Before Mack returned to Christ, he and Phillip had a strained relationship but at least there was some communication. After Mack's divorce to Phillip's mother, that relationship was almost nonexistent. Mack wanted passionately to live life with his son but Phillip wanted no part of it. Cursing him right to his face for destroying his life, Phillip told Mack he would never forgive him for what he did to his mom. The old Mack had never spent much time at home with Phillip or Phillip's mother. In Mack's words, "Hell, I spent most of my time at work trying to keep food on the table and a roof over their heads, but it seems no one remembers that. All they seem to remember is that I was a jerk." Jesus was still helping Mack curb his vocabulary.

Mack took total responsibility for his former failures as a husband, and as a father. Still, his son wanted nothing to do with him. Mack began to recognize Phillip was behaving just as he had behaved when Mack was a boy. He remembered jumping down Phillip's throat for making the smallest mistakes, like forgetting to take out the garbage or turning the lights off in his room when he left for school. Phillip had even once told a friend the only reason he stayed home with the "old man" was because he was loaded. Even though Mack could feel Phillip's hatred toward him, he refused to kick his twenty-year old son out on the street.

Mad Mack's Dangerous Prayer

As usual, when our hearts are supercharged by the love of Christ, our Prayers become Dangerous for those we love. We want them to experience the same love feast we have found in Christ. That's when Mack's heart was crushed for his son. One Sunday after church service, as a bunch of us were hanging out talking in the foyer, Mack and Ted walked up to me. Mack said, with tears in his eyes, "I really want you to pray for my son to come to Christ." He told me Phillip wouldn't listen to him, as he had been a terrible father.

I grabbed another pastor and we held hands with Mack and Ted. I told Mack, "When we pray, we will only have to pray once. We know by the scriptures that God is crazy in love with Phillip and wants to save him." Mack nodded his head in agreement.

This is the Dangerous Prayer we prayed. "Father in Heaven, we thank You for sending Your son Jesus to die for and save Phillip. Satan, we claim Phillip for the kingdom of God in Jesus' name. You can't have him anymore. Father, we ask you to bring someone across Phillip's path that he will listen to. Please send someone that will bring him to You so that he will become a Christ follower. Thank you, Father in Heaven, for always answering our prayers. In Jesus' name, Amen!" It was that simple.

Mack asked, "Now what?"

I simply said, "Now, we celebrate. God heard our prayer and we need to let Him work on it. All we need to do now is thank Him for the answer."

Mack asked, "How long?"

I said, "Until we see the answer."

Mack dropped his head as though he was not convinced. I put my hand on his shoulder and looked him in the eye. "Mack, we just prayed God's will according to His word. There is no way on earth that our prayers will not be answered. God's will is for us to be saved. God said whatever we bind on earth would be bound in Heaven. I'm sure Heaven is working on this. We also asked God to send someone into the field to harvest a soul, Phillip's soul. I have never seen this prayer not answered." With that, he nodded with tears in his eyes and left for lunch.

The Rest of the Story

A few months later, a young man began to visit our church. He found out about our church through a friend and drove an amazing forty-five minutes one way to get there. He continued to come for many weeks. After one particular service, he went down to the altar to rededicate his life to Christ. At that time I was in charge of altar ministry and happened to be serving. I took the young man into a side room and prayed with him, bringing him back to a life with Christ.

A few weeks later, the young man, Ryan, came to a class I was teaching. He had submitted himself to the Holy Spirit's leadership and God had given him an unbridled passion for his friends to come to Christ. The transformation was lopsided with God's love.

After about six months, Ryan brought his best friend to church with him. Initially, his friend was put out by the idea, but through patient persistence, he came. He also came to my class and I was able to pray with him. Over time, the friend became endeared to the Holy Spirit. It may be a surprise to you (though it was not to me) that Ryan's best friend was Phillip, Mack's son. It took around eleven months, but God answered Mack's prayer. Mad Mack became Smiling Mack. He smiled so much it would make your cheeks hurt.

Mack and Phillip's relationship began a restoration process. Eventually, Phillip believed he was called by God to become a minister and with Mack's blessing, Phillip went back to college. He also went to seminary, graduated and became a missionary. He is now married and has a fantastic ministry. His father, Mack, is his biggest financial supporter.

Praying for Others

"You have a choice to make...a world-class Christian or a worldly Christian...world-class Christians know they were... made for a mission" ~Rick Warren, *The Purpose Driven Life*

God wants to free humans from Satan's control. He wants humans to be totally connected in life to Him. Once connected, we can love Him, be a part of His family all over the globe and become like Him in service to others. Once we are His, He wants to use us to reach others through our life, through our Dangerous Prayers. We are God's messengers of love in this world. And like everything with God, it all starts with prayer. When we have His heart and see others with His eyes, we want them to have what we have. As we pray dangerously for others to come to Christ we change, we become a world-class Christian.

When you pray for other people, believe God will listen to you. He has a multitude of ways in playing the cards to help people. He used Phillip's friend who lived almost an hour away to answer Mack's prayer. Boom! Get you some of that!

Praying for others is part of your mission and purpose as an individual. You can't control someone else's mind or their will. Neither will God, but your prayers can truly roam deep behind enemy lines and affect people, especially if you are connected to them by relationship or have influence in their life. Like a husband and a wife, one can pray for the other because they are mutually submitted to God. In a nutshell, your prayers prompt God to influence the hearts of those you pray for.

Ephesians 1:18-19 is a Dangerous Prayer that I have been praying for people for many years:

"I pray that the eyes of your heart may be enlightened in order that you may know the hope to which He has called you, the riches of His glorious inheritance in His holy people, and His incomparably great power for us who believe."

This simply says I am praying they "crack the code" and understand the insider information God has for them, and that they will enjoy a life with the jaw-dropping power of Jesus Christ. I am praying that an insider contact who knows the ropes will cross their path and create a relationship with them so their eyes will be opened to this new life in Christ.

They will go from living without hope to living with hope. That hope comes from the love of God. When the love of God begins to reveal itself, it leads people to the realization that their situation is going to get better. They may not know how, but they know in their spirit it is going to get better. When the life giving power of Jesus Christ shows up in our life, God really begins to do miracles. He answered Mack's prayer for Phillip and had already changed and renewed Mack's own life.

Mack realized there were some things in his life that, as big and successful as he was, he could not fix. Only God could! He always wants to bend over backward to help like sending Phillip's best friend Ryan almost an hour's drive away to help.

Is This New to You?

My guess is either you are a Christ-follower or you picked this book up out of curiosity. Is there a prayer you need answered? You don't need to know Jesus well for Him to answer your prayers. Read the verse from Ephesians again. God is waiting to connect with you.

The next chapter is a story of someone who knew of Jesus but had not met Him yet. What this shrewd leader learned about Jesus in a closed-door meeting caused a shock wave to go through him and filled him with respect and awe, but I'm getting ahead of myself. You can read the story for yourself and see what happened.

PRAYER THREE
The Unfair Advantage

The prayer that allows a human to see like God.

Why Christ followers can see things that no one else can.

There is a darkness that is much worse than the absence of physical light. It's a darkness that keeps you dangerously just out of the reach of truth and just far enough from real life. Jesus said,

"But when your eye is bad, your whole body is filled with darkness. And if the light you think you have is actually darkness, how deep that darkness is!" Matthew 6:23 NLT

In other words we don't know what we don't know, and we can't see what we can't see.

Running In Darkness, A Short Story

"I really don't like being out this late, especially on this side of town. Maybe He'll see me, so the risk of me being seen with Him will be worth my time and trouble." As these thoughts ran through Nicodemus' head, his bodyguard and two closest friends were struggling to keep up with his pace. It didn't occur to him that he was walking so fast he was practically running. He was a man on a mission. A man on a mission to find answers!

As Nicodemus and his friends approached the house, they saw a small crowd milling about the front door. They froze in mid-step and quickly blew out the lights in their two lanterns. They then scurried off the street and stood in the shadows by the side door of an empty house.

After almost an hour, the people were still standing outside talking and carrying on. Nicodemus feeling befuddled, mumbled to his friends and bodyguard, "Why are these people still here? I made myself very clear in my message to Him that I wanted to meet with Him, alone. Maybe He didn't get it? Huh, that's so strange." He shook his head in frustration. "Well, I certainly can't flirt with being seen, so let's just leave and come back at a more favorable time."

Just as the four men lit their lanterns to prepare to leave, a man came out of the front door of the house. He began hugging all the people outside, thanking them for coming and for bringing such a wonderful meal.

Suddenly, the man saw the lights from their lanterns. He finished hugging the last person, then turned in the direction of the lights, walking toward them. He quickened his pace, catching up with them as they were heading out into the street and away from the house; their backs toward him. As the man got closer, he spoke, "Is that you, Nicodemus?"

Hearing that familiar voice, Nicodemus froze in mid-step and slowly turned.

"Oh, it is you Nicodemus! I'm so glad you came. I was expecting you. I thought maybe you had changed your mind but when I saw the lantern lights, I hoped it was you," Jesus said.

"Well, I thought you changed your mind or forgot," said Nicodemus. "When I saw all the people and realized that You were not alone, I decide to leave. We have been waiting for almost an hour."

Jesus' forehead became wrinkled as He said, "I am sorry you had to wait so long. Do you still have time to join me?"

After studying the sincerity in Jesus' face for a moment, Nicodemus said, "Yes, we can stay for a short time."

Returning to the house, Jesus gestured to the four men to enter ahead of him. Once inside, the guests were invited to sit around a large table. An abundance of food and wine remained from the meal Jesus had shared earlier. Jesus apologized. "I'm sorry you missed my friends and family. Please, eat. This is the food and wine they brought to celebrate our visit. I hope you enjoy it."

As everyone began to eat, Jesus asked Nicodemus, "Well, you've come a long way and at this late hour to meet with me. It must be crucially important. How can I help?"

Nicodemus paused. "I've been asking myself the same question ever since I sent the messenger to arrange our meeting." He took a sip of wine to wash down the roast lamb he had begun to nibble on. "I guess you know at this point, not just my name, but also who I am in this community. Perhaps this tells you why I asked for a closed door meeting at night, alone."

Jesus just smiled.

"Teacher," Nicodemus continued, "Like my father and grandfather before me, I have been a Pharisee, leader and teacher in Israel. For over forty-three years, I have seen teachers come and go. Many of them bring some new wobbly insight, hanging around for a while getting everyone jacked up. But eventually they all disappear. Most of these so-called teachers have not been taught by my colleagues in the Sanhedrin nor myself. To be frank, the lack of confidence and power in their words makes them seem nothing more than well-meaning but misguided fools.

"You, however, are different. I have observed You at a safe distance for some time now, in the Temple as well as in the streets of Jerusalem. My friends, here with me, and I know that You are very different from the others we have observed. You possess a master's level savvy. Not only are you a great teacher, but you obviously have God on your side. Otherwise, you could not perform the outrageous miracles that you do. Which, by the way, makes you a dangerous threat to us in the Sanhedrin, but that's not why I'm here. I'm here for myself! I'm seeking understanding. So here's my thought. What I don't understand is why you are different.

"Unless..." Nicodemus seemed confused, but continued, "You are aware that I am a teacher of the scriptures. So I know that only the Messiah is supposed to be able to do the things you do. I'm not willing to say that you are he, but why does God use you to teach? Why is it He helps you perform the miracles you do?" he asked. "Why has He chosen you?"

The Right Question

"Well, Nicodemus, I think you might be asking the wrong question," said Jesus. "Perhaps what you should be asking is, what is it I see that you don't see?"

Nicodemus was silent for a moment. Jesus could tell that maybe this idea had never crossed Nicodemus' mind before.

As Nicodemus and his friends sat there considering Jesus' comment, Jesus said, "The truth is, Nicodemus, there is an invisible Kingdom all around us. And all these amazing things that you hear and see are a result of that Kingdom. I'm just simply operating in a world that you can only see the results of when they manifest in human sight. I see things, know things and do things you cannot see with your natural eyes."

Nicodemus quickly replied, "Then how can I see this invisible Kingdom?"

Jesus answered, "Well, unfortunately you can't, unless you change."

Thinking Jesus was implying that he was not an honorable man, Nicodemus became unexpectedly ticked off. "What do you mean change?" asked Nicodemus. "I've lived the most holy life that was possible since I was a child. I've practically lived at the Temple most of my life and I've loved God and His commandments with all my heart."

Jesus smiled. "Now calm down, my friend. I'm not talking about following a set of rules. This is about being a new person all together. It's about being fresh and new and innocent, like a child. It's about being born all over again." He sat back in his chair to let the impact of His statement do its work while He drank out of His cup.

Nicodemus' face was strained, as though his seventy-three years of life experience was being compressed into a single thought. *How can this be? What does He mean to be born all over again?*

Finally, after what seemed like an eternity of awkward silence, Nicodemus said, "With all due respect, Jesus, I did not come all this way and under these conditions to be made a fool of! What do You mean be born all over again? How can a seventy-three year old man go back into his mother's body? She's ninety-seven years old, by the way! And then she gives birth to me again? To be honest, I cannot believe I'm having this ridiculous conversation with You." Trying to calm himself, he finished his thought. "I expected more. Or at least something that does not defy common sense." He shook his head.

Jesus leaned forward with His elbows on the edge of the table. His guests leaned in slightly, except for Nicodemus, who was now leaning back in his chair, arms folded across his chest.

Jesus looked Nicodemus in the eye for a moment and said, "First, Nicodemus, only humans can have this experience, meaning only those who have passed through the waters of childbirth. It's not for angels or demons, either. It's a second birth, not physical in nature that must take place. When I look at you and your friends here, I don't really see you. I see what you live in. I see your earth suit but you are more than a body with a mind, will and emotion. You are a spirit, first and foremost, and this invisible Kingdom I'm talking about is spiritual."

"But right now, your spirits," He said, as He looked deep into the eyes of each of the four men, "are not in any condition to see this Kingdom that I'm talking about. That is why you must be born all over again. Only God's Spirit can do this for you. How He does it is not easy to understand. It's about as easy as seeing the wind. You can see the wind's effect on things, like trees, or when it kicks up a sand storm, but you can't see the wind itself. " Then slowly, Jesus leaned back into His chair and folded His arms to match Nicodemus.

By the expression on Nicodemus's face, Jesus could tell that he had another question. And sure enough, Nicodemus said, with a little less frustration, "I think I understand what You are saying, but how are these things possible?" This time his tone was different. He was less irritated and more engaged.

The Edge of the Universe

Jesus now focused all His attention on Nicodemus. "How long did you say you have been a Pharisee and a Teacher?" He asked.

"Over forty-three years," Nicodemus said, as he smiled a little sheepishly and was now beginning to feel like a student instead of a teacher.

"And how is it you have been a teacher for so long but you don't understand these things?" Jesus replied, without a single drop of condemnation in His tone.

Then it hit Nicodemus like a ton of bricks. All of a sudden, the unreasonable became reasonable. He thought, *I cannot see it because it is all invisible to my natural eyes. But I could see it with my spiritual eyes if they were working.* Nicodemus was not embarrassed. He was in awe. If age had taught him anything, it was to know when he was about to hear something that would change his life forever. He knew deep inside that he was standing on the edge of the universe, peering into a new dimension. He was about to see things that his ancestors, for thousands of years before him, had only dreamed to see in their lifetime. He was about to see God himself.

Jesus said, "Remember when our ancestor Moses made the bronze snake and mounted it on a tall pole? He lifted it up so our people who had been bitten by poisonous snakes could see it. And do you remember what happened when they looked at the bronzed serpent?"

One of Nicodemus' friends excitedly blurted out, "Yeah, they were healed."

"That's right." Jesus smiled and said, "Well, the same thing will happen to your spirits when you see the Son of Man. One day, He will be lifted up like that bronze serpent and put on a pole for the whole world to see. When this happens, and you, or anyone else looking at him on that pole realizes how much God loves them, then you, and they, will be born all over again," Jesus said.

Jesus took a small sip of wine and sat for a moment staring into His cup, silent, as though He had remembered something. "You see, men," Jesus said, "I have not only lived here on this earth for thirty-one years but I have also lived in Heaven. It is my home, and I remember my Heavenly Father saying how much He loved this world. He said this a very long time ago, even before Adam and Eve. So I am here because of His great love. I am here so that anyone who believes that I am God's Son and will accept what I will soon do for them can have a new spirit and new eyes to see God's Kingdom." Jesus took His last sip of wine and smiled at the speechless men.

The four men just sat there staring at Jesus, as though they had just heard the God of the Universe speak and were totally convinced they had.

"Nicodemus," Jesus said, "this is not about obeying the commandments as you assumed. This is about the love of the Father. It's about the work of God's Spirit, not the work of mere human will or strength. I'm here from Heaven now, to bring the light of understanding about God's Kingdom. Unfortunately, light is useless with eyes that don't see. Nicodemus, your spiritual eyes don't see, and you need new ones," Jesus said.

While their brains were bending over backward to understand the jaw-dropping words they had just heard, the men stood as Jesus got up and walked towards the door. Without a word they gathered the few things they had brought with them, including the lanterns. As they passed one at a time through the door behind Jesus, Jesus turned and looked at Nicodemus and said, "By the way, I never answered your original question."

Nicodemus just stared at Jesus as though it didn't matter.

"Remember? You had asked me how I was able to do the things I do."

All Nicodemus could do was just smile and slowly nod.

"Well, it's a lot like those lanterns you have there. Your journey back home tonight through the darkness will be a lot easier if you light them." Jesus said. "I can see the invisible Kingdom, so I see and hear what my father in Heaven does and says. So I just do what He says and it happens. It's not that hard when you can see."

Nicodemus said, "So when I see you lifted up, I will be able to have these new eyes too?"

"Yes, Nicodemus," Jesus said. "It is the Father's will to give you the ability to see and hear the Kingdom as well."

"When will this happen?" asked Nicodemus.

"Sooner than you think, my friend. Sooner than you think!" said Jesus as he smiled, stepped in and closed the door.

How Do You See Now?

"Imagine a lot of people who have always lived in the dark. You come and try to describe to them what light is like. You might tell them that if they come into the light that same light would fall on them all, and they would all reflect it and thus become what we call visible." ~ C.S. Lewis, *Mere Christianity*

I wear glasses, and each time I go to the optometrist the process is pretty much the same. They ask a few general health questions and then check my eyesight with various tests. After reviewing the eye chart, they ask me to rest my forehead against the viewfinder and proceed to change the lenses until I can identify the one that enables me to see the clearest for each eye. When the correct lens is put before the correct eye, jackpot! What a difference! The world suddenly comes into focus, and I can see every little detail with minute clarity.

Unfortunately, our natural eyes can only see the effects of the spiritual world but not the spiritual world itself. However, human spirits can see the spirit world when they become born again. This was Jesus' whole message to Nicodemus. And only Holy Spirit can transform a person's life to be able to "see" the Kingdom of God. That Kingdom is a place we can't see with the human eye but it's where God lives and rules.

Earth is not ruled exclusively by God at this time but will be in the near future. His power in the earth is performed through Holy Spirit in the lives of Christ-followers, as they live in communion with God. This is done through continual prayer. Communion is a continual flow of love, thoughts, ideas, and direction from God in Heaven through Holy Spirit into our conscious mind. This is what I call spiritual intuition.

Online

I don't know much about computers but I do know mine works better when it's online. With Facebook, Yahoo, Google and another million websites to resource, any computer without the capacity to connect to the Internet is functionally obsolete. Yes, you can type documents with Word, create spreadsheets in Excel and even do amazing art with Adobe, all without being online.

However, most of these software applications need either online verification or regular updates from their developers to keep them current and relevant. One online vendor that provides storage for audio and video files calls the servers where the files are stored, the "cloud". So, access to these files requires my computer to have the software ability to communicate online, therefore an Internet connection is still needed.

The Mind of Christ and Holy Spirit

This computer metaphor is perfect to describe how Christ followers connect with Father God in Heaven through prayer. Check out what the Apostle Paul said almost two thousand years ago and see if you see what I see.

"That is what the scriptures mean when they say, 'No eye has seen, no ear has heard, and no mind has imagined what God has prepared for those who love Him.'

But it was to us that God revealed these things by His Spirit, for His Spirit searches out everything and shows us God's deep secrets. No one can know a person's thoughts except that person's own spirit and no one can know God's thoughts except God's own Spirit. And we have received God's Spirit (not the world's spirit), so we can know the wonderful things God has freely given us.

When we tell you these things, we do not use words that come from human wisdom. Instead, we speak words given to us by the Spirit, using the Spirit's words to explain spiritual truths. But people who aren't spiritual can't receive these truths from God's Spirit. It all sounds foolish to them and they can't understand it, for only those who are spiritual can understand what the Spirit means. Those who are spiritual can evaluate all things but they cannot be evaluated by others. For, who can know the Lord's thoughts? Who knows enough to teach Him? But we understand these things, for we have the mind of Christ." 1 Corinthians 2:9-16 NLT

Being born all over again creates the capacity for our human spirits to receive and understand what's on God's mind when we pray. We have a mind that is like Christ, who understands the continual flow of information back and forth between Him and God the Father, through Holy Spirit. You might say our "software" is compatible to Holy Spirit's and Father God's.

Will This Be Debit or Credit?

As Nicodemus was leaving, he asked Jesus when all of this might take place. Jesus answered, "When you see the Son of Man being lifted up." Jesus was explaining that the new "software" he was going to receive one day when he was born all over again was going to cost big bucks. Just like anything really life-changing, the initial development cost is enormous. The years and millions of man hours that have gone into developing technological equipment like computers and software can be overwhelming, not to mention much too expensive for any single individual to afford.

But someone has to pay the monster-sized bill!

When I go to Best Buy to pick out a new computer or connect to the Internet for the first time, I have to answer a question: "Will this be debit or credit?" Jesus, by his death, paid for all this amazing stuff. He set up a credit account that has been fully funded just for us. Our equipment (our new Spirit in Christ) and software (The Mind of Christ) is paid for and is waiting to be installed. Also our "Internet provider", the Holy Spirit, is ready to connect us with Heaven for a continual flow of divine love, inspiration, spiritual insight and power from our Father God. This is called prayer, and it's the most Dangerous Prayer anyone could ever pray!

Like Google!

Like everything else, it's not over 'til the paperwork is done or at least some type of commitment. Even though Jesus Christ paid for all this amazing stuff, we must let Him know that we really want it and are not just shopping around. So, He requires us to make it personal by filling out the request ourselves, which means it comes from our heart. No one else is allowed to fill out the form for us.

And like Google, it's very simple: All we do is fill in the blank by telling God what we want. We want Jesus to be our Lord and Savior. We check the box on the agreement by accepting that Jesus paid the monster-sized price by dying for all our sins. We then press "send" by saying "Amen", which means, "Let it be so." The order is sent, and we get tapped into the God of the Universe with explosive power!

By the way, this is pretty much explained in Romans 10:9-10 NLT.

"If you confess with your mouth that Jesus is Lord and believe in your heart that God raised Him from the dead, you will be saved. For it is by believing in your heart that you are made right with God and it is by confessing with your mouth that you are saved."

Shopping Cart

"Once we accept our limits, we go beyond them."

~Albert Einstein

So, how about you? Do you want God to always answer your prayers? Don't be afraid! Go ahead fill out the paperwork and hit "send". It's simple. Pray the following prayer when you are ready and you will have "new eyes" just like Nicodemus eventually received.

Here's the Dangerous Prayer:

"God, this is (insert your name here). I want Jesus to be my Lord and Savior. Thank you for sending Him to pay the monster- sized price so I may become a Christ follower. Please make me new and fill me with the Holy Spirit. I look forward to being spiritually tapped in with your brand-spanking-new eyes to see your Kingdom. In Jesus name. Amen."

It's pretty simple because God always answers your prayers!

By the way, tell another believer what you did and see what happens. This decision is meant to be shared!

All We Need Is A Miracle

When I was eighteen years old, I needed a miracle. Actually, someone else needed a miracle but they asked me to help. Just about two years before, I had prayed the Dangerous Prayer above. If I hadn't prayed, I wouldn't have been able to "see" with different eyes to help with the miracle. But because of a simple yet Dangerous Prayer, you won't believe what happened next. It was strangely vicious, in a good way.

PRAYER FOUR
The Invisible Law of Agreement

The reason God cannot do anything He wants to do, and why He needs your help.

Eighteen-Year-Old Minister

In August of 1979, I had preached for a week in a small church near Shallotte, North Carolina. While standing around chatting after the second night, a lady by the name of Lois approached me and asked me to go to her home that night and pray for her mother. Lois' mother had been diagnosed by the doctor as having hardening of the arteries also called atherosclerosis. This was a common, treatable disorder but in her case was caught at a very late stage. The majority of her arterial walls were so built up with plaque that they were actually stiff and so badly blocked that her blood flow was reduced to barely keeping her alive. Freaked out a little, I agreed to go with Lois and pray for her mom.

Arriving at Lois's home, I saw a number of people already there whom I had seen at the church earlier. After a few greetings, I went into the room to meet Lois's mother and was shocked at what I saw.

Her mother was strapped to the bed. She was skin and bones and her body was jerking uncontrollably and violently at times. Her eyes were sunk deep into her head. She looked like a living skeleton. Discreetly, I asked Lois what the doctors were doing for her mother's condition. She smiled at me, with peace in her eyes, and told me the doctor said her condition was beyond hope of treatment. She added that the few options available were very costly and really didn't offer much hope anyway due to her advanced condition. She told me they brought her home from the hospitable to be comfortable, and she was grateful that I was there. The last part of her comment gave me pause.

With forced confidence, I asked Lois what she expected of me. I had a sense that she was counting on me for something I was not sure I could deliver. She said that she and her siblings had been praying for her mom for some time. They were in agreement and believed that God would heal her, even though she was in her late seventies and in this condition. She believed that her mom was not only going to be healed but would also be with them for many more years to come.

The Agreement

"Single mind must be master, else there will be no agreement in anything." ~Abraham Lincoln

As Lois was speaking, I looked from her to her mother. To be honest, I was surprised that she was expectant of her mother's healing. I was also concerned that she thought I, a young, new minister, could bring about the results she anticipated. She smiled at me and said all she wanted was for me to pray in agreement with them that her mom would be healed.

In agreement? Could I really pray, honestly, in agreement with them? I looked at the lady on the bed again. I turned to Lois and asked if this is truly what the family believed. Her siblings were beginning to gather in the bedroom with us, smiling at me, as though they knew something I didn't know.

At that moment I began to feel the weight of this responsibility settle on my eighteen-year-old shoulders. I had only been a minister for about a year, with very little training. Most of my ministry work up until this moment had been public speaking, youth evangelism and teaching small groups. Miracles were not on my list of proficiencies at that time but it didn't seem to bother Lois one bit. See, Lois knew what the Bible said, and she was in agreement with it.

"Are any of you sick? You should call for the elders of the church to come and pray over you, anointing you with oil in the name of the Lord. Such a prayer offered in faith will heal the sick and the Lord will make you well. And if you have committed any sins, you will be forgiven." James 5:14-15 NLT

Persistence

Lois could tell I was both nervous and hesitant but she was persistent. She said that she and her sisters and brother were confident that their mother would be healed and that all we needed to do was to pray the prayer of faith, in agreement. The first thing that ran through my head was *Why me?* However, looking into the eyes of this woman who had so much faith, I didn't have the heart to verbalize it. Still, I wondered why they had waited. Why hadn't they already done this if they really believed she would be healed? Why was I going to be the one to lead what honestly looked like a lost cause? I was frightened of this whole situation. Still, I was there as the minister and needed to do my job, regardless of how I felt it would turn out.

I looked at the folks gathered in the room and tried to seem very confident and spiritual like, *no sweat, I've got this.* I eventually got the nerve to ask everyone to gather around the bed and hold hands so I could pray for God to heal the woman. I took Lois's hand, and as I reached for her mother's hand, it was jerking so badly I could barely hold it steady. Everyone else in the room began to hold hands until we had formed a circle around the bed.

As I looked into Lois' mother's eyes, I felt so much compassion for her. My heart broke for her condition and for those in the room who loved her so much. Surprised that they would ask an eighteen-year-old kid to come and pray for her, I was honored, afraid, and sad, all at the same time. *God, please let this work.*

As I opened my mouth to pray, something happened. I felt a presence in the room. I wasn't sure what it was at the time. There was a power there that I later understood to be Holy Spirit. Not only was He there, I could sense Him doing what we could not do and certainly what I could not do, which was heal this woman. Up until that moment, I really thought it would be best to just release the lady into the Lord's hands to take her to Heaven. I thought it would be better for her to be in Heaven and not to stay in that condition. But that was not my decision. It was the decision of those who were her family and who had faith.

After I finished praying for her healing, we all wiped the tears from our eyes, giving each other a hug, knowing something happened but not knowing what. I left, never returning to that home again. However, I did get word that the lady not only recovered but she gained almost thirty pounds of her weight back. And though she still used a walker to get around, that following winter she made four quilts, which you cannot do if you cannot control your body's motor functions. Amazingly, she lived in very good health many more years after that.

It Only Takes Two

"Alone we can do so little; together we can do so much."
~Helen Keller

Through this experience as a young Baptist minister, I learned that this bold and dangerous kind of praying affects Heaven and Earth. It's secret is the power of agreeing with God first.

Jesus said to him, "As far as possibilities goes, everything is possible for the person who believes." Mark 9:23 GWT

It was certainly not my faith alone, which was very small if any, but the way we collectively connected to our Father in Heaven and allowed Holy Spirit to heal Lois' mom. It was the faith of her children. That's when I realized why they had those smiles on their faces and the quiet confidence in their spirits. They understood that God always answers Dangerous Prayers of agreement. I didn't get this beyond what it meant to me in my head. They actually had the faith in their hearts that when we prayed, God would heal their mother. And that made all the difference.

"Again I say to you, that if two of you will agree in the earth about any matter which they will request, it will be done for them from the presence of my Father who is in Heaven." Matthew 18:19 ABPE

Their agreement in prayer was not academic for them. It was real. It was dangerous. They saw something inside their hearts that I did not see in mine. They saw their mother getting out of bed and living her life as she had in the past. And that is exactly what happened, but not everyone prays Dangerous Prayers that cause Heaven to respond.

Prepare yourself. What I'm about to share next is not for the faint of heart and may even upset you, until God gives you your own understanding of it.

1994

When I was thirty-three years old, I was asked by Tim, another pastor in our church, to go with him to the home of a lady who had terminal cancer. We were to pray for her to be healed. I agreed and went along with Tim as spiritual support. On the way to the lady's home, Tim began to tell me a little about her. She was young, in her early thirties. This disease had hit her very quickly and in less than a year, she was considered terminal. Her name was Diane and her husband was John. Diane and John had a five-year-old son named Troy. John was in gut-wrenching agony over the thought of not only losing his wife but the mother of his young son. Diane's oncologist was not giving her much hope for the treatments due to the advanced growth and stage of the cancer.

When we arrived, we were met at the door by a dazed John. Though he was trying to be positive, he looked hopeless. We were led into the family room where we met his son, Troy, a handsome and buoyant young boy with black hair like his dad and dark brown eyes like his mom. He had such a nice smile. Diane was on the couch, which had been turned into a bed with lots of pillows and blankets. On the end table next to the couch were three prescription bottles and a couple of half-full glasses. Beside the couch on the floor was a plastic-lined waste can, which had recently been used for catching whatever meds or liquids Diane could not keep down.

As we entered, she was trying to make herself look more presentable by pulling back her hair and sitting up on the pillows.

She apologized for the condition of the house. I told her we were there to see her, not to buy the house. She smiled painfully and thanked us for coming. Her husband and son sat at her feet while we sat in two leather recliners. Tim tried to create small talk. After a few minutes of getting to know them, Diane and her husband began to reiterate what my friend had told me about her disease on the way to their house. They would talk in code when saying anything that might upset Troy. Both Diane and John struggled to not break down and sob, as they took us through the last year's events of doctor visits and test reports. It was obvious that fear had totally gripped them, even though they were Christians. I was angry at this disease for devouring this beautiful family but tried not to let it show.

After a short while, Tim looked over toward me. It was then that I realized why I was there. I leaned forward on the edge of my recliner and began to ask a few questions about their faith, to try to find where they were in their relationship with God. Both told me they were Christians and had been since their childhood. They told me the name of the Christian church they grew up in. They said they believed in prayer but had not been the ones to call us to their home. A friend had mentioned our church and recommended that they have pastors from our church come out and pray with them. So, they had not set up the meeting. Our meeting was prearranged by the friend not present.

After a few more minutes of discussion, I began to explain to them that God would answer their prayers as long as they asked with faith in their hearts. I added that it was also very important that they were both in agreement. After explaining the passage in Matthew 18:19 and discussing a few other verses, I asked if they had any questions. They responded that they did not. I asked if I could pray with them for her healing and they agreed.

We stood and held hands, surrounding Diane. I anointed her with oil and prayed for her to be healed. We all said "Amen," together, including handsome little Troy. I thought things went well, and I was expecting a great report from the doctor in the near future. We chatted for a bit and then said our goodbye and left.

Shocked

It was about six weeks later that I asked my pastor friend, Tim, if he had heard how Diane was doing. He said that he had not. Since she was a regular member of another church, he had not heard anything new. He said he would touch base with his friend who had set up the appointment. Later that night, Tim called to give me the sad news; Diane had died just a few weeks after we had prayed for her.

What? That can't be true! But it was. Diane was dead.

I was shocked and full of questions! I asked Tim to go by just to check on her husband. Even though they had a church and pastor, I wanted to see if we could be of any additional help with meals or help around the house. The next day Tim reported that though John and Troy were obviously devastated by Diane's death and they were doing as well as could be expected. I was still shocked and very angry. Why didn't God heal Diane? It was then that Tim told me something that floored me. He had found out that Diane and John had started their relationship some eight years earlier by having an affair. Both Diane and John were married at the time and their affair destroyed two families. Tim went on to say that Diane had confessed to John that she felt like her disease was a curse from God because of their affair and that she would never be forgiven. What a big lie!

When I heard this, I was heartbroken because I also remembered their religious beliefs. They both were raised with a religious belief that supported what Diane said. So with her own mouth, she declared what she believed. Had I known this, before praying for her healing, I would have spent much more time teaching them about the love and forgiveness offered to them by the Lord Jesus. You see, Diane had conflicting beliefs. She had been seduced by the enemy using religion to slip in the back door, set her up, and kill her through disease.

Diane's desire to be healed was in opposition to her belief that the sickness was a curse from God. She could not agree with God for forgiveness or healing. This was a lie! Nevertheless, how could she believe that the same God who had sent this curse on her was the God who was going to heal her? Inside her heart, she had to choose. The curse won over God's love.

The Difference

In 1979, Lois and her family were in strong agreement and were very clear on what God's Word said about healing, to the point that a young and very inexperienced eighteen-year-old minister prayed with them, and God answered their Dangerous Prayer. I was thirty-three years old when I prayed with John and Diane and had seen many miracles by that time, but my experience and faith in God's desire to heal Diane was not as strong as Diane's dangerous belief about her "curse". This comment is not in any way a condemnation of Diane. I believe today she is with Jesus in Heaven. She was just not at a place in her life at the time where she could be in agreement with God to heal her while on earth.

The Dangerous Part of Prayer Agreement

"Can two people walk together without agreeing on the direction?" Amos 3:3 NLT

I want to be clear on this; agreement is not something God uses as a measuring tool of how holy we are! Agreement is simply God's way of working with our will. God honors our will so much that He is prepared to let us decide for ourselves, even when He knows that our decisions may harm us. Because He loves us, He has done everything possible to give us all the information (the Bible) and inspiration (Holy Spirit) possible to help us agree with Him so that He may answer our prayers. He's not a tyrant, nor will He just do anything He wants to in our lives. God is not in control of everything, especially what we decide for our own lives. This kind of thinking will get you killed. If that were not true, He would just say the word and everyone would be instantly new creatures in Christ and everyone would go to Heaven immediately. But even salvation as we know it requires being in agreement with God.

"If you confess with your mouth the Lord Jesus and believe in your heart that God has raised Him from the dead, you will be saved. For with the heart one believes unto righteousness and with the mouth confession is made unto salvation." Romans 10:9-10 NKJV

After reflecting upon Lois' mother and Diane's situation, I realized that I could not force anyone to believe and agree with God. All I could do was to share what God's word said and allow each person to decide for him or herself what he or she would believe in and agree with God. Now, when I pray with people, I spend time trying to find out what they really believe will happen when we pray. Only if their belief is

Biblical can we be in agreement and expect what Jesus said in that passage in Matthew 18:19.

Filling the Gaps

God wants to be in every decision of our lives, not just the big ones, but the small decisions as well. Living and praying in agreement with God honors Him and gives Him a chance to help us with those decisions we just cannot see from His global point of view. There are always "gaps" of understanding that need to be filled in order for us to pray and follow God's leading. Like my story in the next chapter, the answer to one of my Dangerous Prayers was literally in front of me every day when I would go to work, but I couldn't see it until God filled in the "gap."

PRAYER FIVE
GPS

God's Positioning System. How God gets you from where you are to where you need to be.

Road Trip

Many years ago I was a lay minister and gave my time to the church without compensation. I did that for over eighteen years. During part of those years, I owned a small company that contracted phases of the assembly processes from other companies. One summer my contracts were brutally low. I had been praying dangerously for more business so I would not have to have to lay off part of our workforce. At the time I was also doing most of the new business development for our company. I sensed in my prayer time to call again on a contact that in the past had not produced any business for our company. I was seriously hoping this time would be different.

When I called this contact, he actually invited me to have a meeting with him in his office, which I did. I was cautiously optimistic. In our meeting, he discussed the recent changes and expansion that his company had been experiencing and needed our services. So, we discussed what services he believed he was going to need and wrapped up the meeting with the information he had at the time. He said he would call in the next couple of weeks with more specific information. As weeks kept coming and going with no phone call, I decided to drop by his office and face up to where he was with our potential contract good or bad.

As soon as I rounded the corner that led to his office, he was smiling and apologizing at the same time for not getting back to me sooner. He said I would get a call that night from one of his associates with the balance of the details. This would allow us to finalize the paperwork and get started. True to his word, that night I got a call from his associate in Colorado, and I was able to put a proposal together. They accepted it within three days.

What a great answer to my prayer. Not only did this new contract help us keep existing employees but because it was so jaw-droppingly larger than we originally discussed, it required additional employees, which I hired from the church I was attending. Dangerous Prayer answered—yes!

But I'm getting a little ahead of myself.

Entering Destination

After the initial calculations for this contract, I realized how grossly understaffed and underfunded I was. So I created a crazy list of specific needs to accomplish this contract, and I began to pray my next Dangerous Prayer. One of my personal fears that caused me to break out in a cold sweat had been the fear of failure. What if I promised something and wasn't able to deliver it on time? I would be toast! In the business world, you just don't do that because of potential loss in revenue for the customer, not to mention the loss of integrity and the possible legal ramifications. So I was staring this massive opportunity in the face, unsure I could pull it off. I had pride and money on the line.

One of my many small mountains to climb in taking on this new opportunity was the need for additional operations and warehouse space. I needed an additional 8,000 square feet and did not know where to find it at a reasonable price, especially in such a short time. As I continued to go through my list of logistics for the job, I found I needed a forklift, a break room with a phone for employees, vending machines, ample restrooms, ample parking, a security system and truck docks. I needed all of this within a week. Did I say a week? Yep! One week! Oh yeah, I also failed to mention that I needed thousands of dollars to pay my new employees until I received payment from my client, which would not happen for at least thirty days after the first deliveries.

"Turn Left At The Next Traffic Sign."

A few mornings later, I was in my in my office, dangerously praying over this list of things I needed. There was still a boatload to do in order to accomplish the answer to that first prayer, which was to bring in more work for my company. Then it hit me. Out of the blue, the Holy Spirit prompted me to get into my truck and start driving.

What?

Yeah, go get in your truck. Now!

I had never done anything like this before. To get in my truck and drive just because I felt prompted by God was not the most urgent thing on my list to do, but I did it.

As I came to the first traffic sign on my journey, I asked Holy Spirit, "Okay...which way?" As odd as it may sound, I sensed *turn left,* so I did. I soon came to a fork in the road and again was prompted to go left. I kept doing this for many miles at stop signs and traffic lights until I was sitting at one particular very busy traffic light. I had intended to go straight, until I looked over to the left and saw a large brick manufacturing facility.

I remember saying to God, "That is just what I need. It would be perfect if they had space in that building." As soon as I said these words out loud, I heard in my heart, *Why don't you go and ask?* The next thought that came to my mind was,

How would my request sound to another sane business person?

I almost kept driving straight through the light.

"Redirecting. One Moment, Please"

You can imagine the mental struggle I was having about this whole process. In the business world, most of the items I needed cost a lot of money and usually required large financial deposits in advance, as well as a long-term lease and commitment. At this time, my company was not in any position to make these commitments. To go and negotiate for these items would take a miracle. In the middle of my mental gymnastics, Holy Spirit broke in and I was reminded of a verse in the Bible. It was Philippians 4:19 NLT.

"And this same God who takes care of me will supply all your needs from His glorious riches, which have been given to you in Christ Jesus."

So now was the time to either be guided by my feelings and fears, or be led by Holy Spirit and God's Word. I gritted my teeth, chose the latter, and decided to pull into the parking lot and enter the building.

Entering the reception area, I spoke to a lady who, with a cleverly-disguised smile on her face, did not seem very happy to see me. This did not help my self-confidence. After I told her who I was and the name of my company, I told her I was looking for some additional space to lease. I added that I noticed how large their facility was and asked if they would have any operational and warehouse space available.

She did not smile or address my concern, but only said, "You will need to talk to the general manager." She directed me to the waiting area just outside his imposing office door, which was partially open. As I took my seat, she went into his office and quickly returned. She continued with that cleverly-disguised smile and said, "It may take a while."

At least he had agreed to see me. Sweet!

As I sat in the waiting area, I continued to pray. I thanked the Lord for always answering my Dangerous Prayers. I knew I was on a journey to receive the answer to my prayers. I also knew that if I did not get discouraged and give up, I would see His miraculous hand working on my behalf. I blatantly smiled to myself as I sat. I chose at that time to believe God was working all things together for my good, even though I had no idea how it would all play out.

The imposing door to the general manager's office was still partially open, and I could hear him on the phone having a discussion. I leaned forward and caught a glimpse of his face and his desk. He was in his mid-forties, with graying, sandy blond hair, and was wearing rimless glasses. He was not smiling at all. His desk was piled high with overstuffed folders. As I slowly leaned back in my chair, I realized he was under as much stress as I was, poor guy. So I began to pray for him to have peace and that God would help him with his work. Although I had never met him before, I felt a good bit of empathy for him.

Shortly after my prayer for him, the door to his office swung open. Out walked a tall, thin man wearing dark suit pants and a light blue dress shirt, sleeves rolled up, and no tie. He walked up to me and smiled with perfect white teeth. As he stuck out his hand to greet me, he said, "My name is Jeff, and I'm the general manager here."

As I shook his hand, my whole mood changed. He was very warm and friendly. He ushered me into his office, cleaned some files off a chair in front of his desk and asked what he could do for me. I explained who I was and what my company did, as well as my need for the additional facility space. I told him I had just been riding by his building and wondered if he had any additional space here. I also half jokingly mentioned all the other things I needed, like the forklift, restrooms, break room with snack machines, telephone, truck docks, and alarm systems, all for a great price and terms. He was leaning back in his chair with his hands together on his chest as in a meditative state, yet his eyes were fixed on me.

"Follow Me."

After I finished the description of my needs, Jeff smiled with a glint in his eye, stood up, and said, "Please follow me."

We immediately left his office and headed down a long, wide hallway. After passing a few smiling employees, we turned and walked through swinging doors, entering a world of cloth. Apparently, this company Jeff worked for bought large rolls of woven fabric and converted them down to small rolls to be sold in their chain of fabric piece good stores. We walked all over this very old building as he began to explain what each department did. I met mostly ladies who seemed to be very happy with their job, including their boss, Jeff.

After about a twenty-minute tour and many greetings and introductions, we wound up back at the main entrance of the building near his office. Jeff looked at me and said, "As you can see, we are all filled up. We use every inch of our 65,000 square feet." He paused for a moment and said, "Please excuse me for a second." He stepped into his secretary's office and told her that he would be back shortly. And with that, he walked by me and said, "Let's go," as he proceeded to walk out the front doors of the building. He walked very fast and headed straight for the parking lot. He never said a word but just got in his vehicle closed the door and cranked it up. I took his cue and hurried to get in mine to follow him.

En Route

As I followed him, I was praying and asking God to give me wisdom. I prayed this would not be a waste, because time was running out for me. If something didn't happen soon, I would not be ready to accept delivery of the product components for our new contract. Jeff seemed very friendly and acted like he wanted to help me but I was bumfuzzled about the "tour" he had just given me back at his other facility. I told God that I trusted Him to provide even if this was a wild goose chase.

I followed his blue pickup truck for about three miles before we turned left into an office/warehouse industrial park. He continued to the end of the main drive then pulled up to very large metal building. It looked to me to be thirty to forty thousand square feet. What was odd to me as I pulled into the parking lot was there were only two cars parked there.

The building did not have a lobby or visitor entrance, only a metal door. The door had to be opened with a key after disarming the security system with a keypad beside the door. My curiosity got the best of me and as we entered the building, I asked him what they did in such a large building with only two employees. He looked at me, smiled and said, "Follow me and I'll show you." I could tell that Jeff was enjoying himself. I was so distracted by his answer that I paid very little attention to the minimal lighting in the building.

After coming from bright sunshine outside, I could barely see. All I could tell was that it was a huge facility. As we walked, my eyes began to adjust to the light. I began to see, through the shadows, very large stacks of bins and boxes that almost reached the twenty-foot ceiling. The lighting was so dim that as we walked through the aisles created by the stacks, I almost walked into a steel column. Fortunately, Jeff saw it before I did and warned me. From that point on, I decided to walk behind him, not beside him, until we got to where we were going. This place could be dangerous.

As we came to what I thought was the farthest part of the building and about to drop off the edge of the world, Jeff opened a door and my eyes were immediately stabbed with blinding light. I stepped through the door and was introduced to Betty and Liz. After a little small talk, Jeff explained they were the only two employees in the building and that their safety was of his utmost concern. Betty and Liz converted larger spools of lace onto smaller spools to be sold in the company's stores. After a brief explanation of their work hours, we walked back toward the main door. This time I made sure to look out for that deadly column!

It's very surreal what happens when we pray Dangerous Prayers and push through our fears to trust Holy Spirit to help us find our way.

"Approaching Destination."

As Jeff and I approached the exit we had entered about twenty minutes earlier, he stopped and said, "Stay here for a sec and I'll go turn on the lights."

Since I could barely see in the dim light, I did not argue. Jeff was only gone about ninety seconds when the whole building lit up. As my eyes were again adjusting, I realized just how large this dang facility really was. Man, it was big! I was standing in front of four loading docks. Jeff quickly appeared from behind a stack of boxes and said, "How many square feet did you say you needed?" I told him 8,000 would be great, but I could get by with 6,000, if I had a forklift. I knew I could take advantage of the height of the ceiling by stacking some of my materials. He stood and looked around for a moment and said, "I believe between these four columns we have about 6800 square feet." Then he said, "Come over here. I want to show you something." We walked around a stack of boxes up to a brand spanking new forklift with the keys in it. He said, "Will this do?"

I just stared for a moment at the forklift like a kid on Christmas morning. I smiled so big my cheeks hurt later, but I eventually said, "You bet it will." Then he showed me a fully appointed break room with canteen equipment, a telephone and restrooms.

All I could think was, *This is perfect*, but then reality sneaked up on me from behind, and I thought, *This is gonna cost a fortune*. So I turned to Jeff, who was looking like Santa Claus to me and said, "This is perfect. It's exactly what I need, with every detail."

Jeff smiled from ear to ear and said, "I'm glad I could help."

Then I sheepishly asked, while holding my breath, how much he wanted for it on a monthly basis.

Jeff answered, "How much do you want to pay?"

As I slowly began to breathe, I thought about his question. How much do I want to pay? I smiled and said, "How about $250 per month?"

He smiled back, stuck out his hand, and said, "It's a deal."

I looked at him and his outstretched hand in absolute shock. But before he changed his mind, I quickly shook his hand and asked if he had a lease for me to sign. He said to just send him something on letterhead. Wow! What a sweet deal!

God's Positioning System

If I had not spent so much time that day with Jeff and all his employees (that he treated like close family), I would have thought God had sent him as an angel...well, he kind of did, but I knew Jeff was human like the rest of us, even though he was such a blessing to me: a real miracle. I was glad I was connected to GPS (God's Positioning System) with perfect alignment.

Another Dangerous Prayer answered!

I went home with a huge smile on my face and a grateful heart for God directing my every step. I also learned a lot about prayer that day. I learned that I needed to trust in the Lord with all my heart and not just trust my own understanding. I also learned to listen and follow His instructions, even if they sometimes didn't make a lot of sense, like getting into my vehicle and expecting Holy Spirit to guide me to the answers I needed. He certainly made it simple for me, just like it says in Proverbs:

"Trust in the LORD with all your heart; do not depend on your own understanding. Seek His will in all you do, and He will show you which path to take." Proverbs 3:5,6 NLT

I would have been stuck and not able to take advantage of the Dangerous Prayer God had already answered if I had not trusted Him to guide my steps. I haven't even told you how He answered my prayer for the thousands of dollars to pay my employees. No one gave me the money, and I did not borrow a dime, either. Well, maybe another time I'll tell you about *that* Dangerous Prayer.

Where Do You Need To Go?

"Be sure you put your feet in the right place, then stand firm." ~Abraham Lincoln

I know this may sound oversimplified, but I believe after years of following God and experiencing Him answer my Dangerous Prayers, you can have your Dangerous Prayers answered if you will just be a little gutsy and follow Him. Holy Spirit will guide you just like an internal Global Positioning System (GPS).

He is no respecter of persons. I'm not any more special than you. Maybe a little more crazy but that's another story. Ask Him for guidance and get out there and go. Go make your phone call, start writing your letter, take your trip, launch your business, ask your loved one you've been mean to for your forgiveness. Do whatever it is you are deathly afraid you will fail at but know inside that you need to do.

Say it out loud. "God, I'm trusting you to direct my every step. I believe with all my heart that You always answer my Dangerous Prayers."

God will not let you down. He never has, and He won't start with you. You only have to stay with it until you have it. Listen to God every step of your way and trust Him. And for God's sake and yours, don't quit in the middle of Him guiding you to your answer, or you could miss out big time!

Right now, write down your prayer request and your next step. Then, do what you know you need to do. Put the book down and do it now. Don't read on until you have taken your next step. Now smile real big, because you know in your heart I'm right.

By the way, the building Jeff let me lease space from was right across the street in front of my business. The answer to my Dangerous Prayer was staring me in the face every day. Your answer is probably closer than you think, too!

Right Out of the Blue

I didn't write this book to entertain you, although as I was editing it, I've laughed a lot while reliving some of the parts. But I wrote it to help you get your Dangerous Prayers answered. I'm keenly aware of the tough things we can go through that aren't our doing. Like my friend Gary, who was sued for millions of dollars right out of the blue. He never believed something like that could have happened to him. But he believed that God would answer his Dangerous Prayer, and that made all the difference.

PRAYER SIX
Specific Desire

Stop praying "If it be thy will..." prayers. Those can get you killed. God is moved by specific, passionate desire.

The $2,500,000 Letter

Gary had gotten another letter from his insurance company—the one that insured his business. This one was different. This time he found out that most of the other subcontractors he had worked with were out of business, and he could be next on the list for extinction if this vicious threat had its way. Up until now, Gary was not concerned. He was a man of God. He honored God by running his business in a way that not only pleased God but also brought honor to His name. He had a strong work ethic and lived a principled life. But now, he was concerned. Years of hard work, sacrifice and integrity could go right down the tubes.

A few days after the letter, the Sheriff's Department arrived and Gary was served a subpoena. Now it was up close and personal.

He was officially being sued. They were not just suing his company but were also attempting to sue him personally. Lori, Gary's wife, had been leading a Bible study when she got the news. She was not the worrywart that Gary was but now she was concerned too. They had never been sued before. What did this all mean? And why was it happening to them?

For weeks before the trial date, Gary met with attorneys discussing the situation, trying to decide the best course of action to take.

This whole ordeal was instantly traumatizing, and he could not even think straight. *Do we just negotiate it out? Is that what you do in these situations? Surely you don't just go head to head in a courtroom. What if I lose? I could lose everything. I don't have 2.5 million dollars to pay the plaintiff.* These thoughts kept running through Gary's mind over and over. *I'm innocent! I did not do anything. I bet they are thinking, Yeah, that's what they all say.* It all sounded and felt like something from a bad horror flick.

Ask For Directions

"I know your actions, that you are neither cold nor hot. I wish you were cold or hot." Revelations 3:15 ISV

Lori could see the monster-sized weight of the pending hearing bearing down on her husband whom she loved dearly.

He was carrying around the mental burden of all the details of the pending trial and not sharing them with her as he usually would. She knew he did not want to trouble her with them, but this was not how they operated in their marriage.

Finally, she told him that he needed some help with this massive burden. He had already hired legal counsel, and they had prayed for God's will to be done. What did his wife expect? What else was there to do except endure it "like a man?" Well, since most men aren't good at stopping and asking for directions or help, Lori decided to recommend that Gary talk to someone. Someone he could talk to about the spiritual weight and impact this firestorm was having on him. She recommended he come see me.

It was a Friday, about a week before the trial when Gary came by my office. He was as warm and friendly as always but I could see some wear of concern on his face. After we sat and caught up a bit, I asked him what I could do for him. He proceeded to bring me up to speed about the lawsuit. He also said that he was very distraught at the possibility of losing, even though he had done nothing wrong. I asked if had he and Lori talked much about it, and he said he was trying to keep most of the daily details to himself so as not to worry her. Yes, they had talked. As a result, he called to meet with me.

After a few more details from Gary, I leaned forward and said, "What do you want?"

He looked at me for a moment as though I had not heard a thing he had said in the last forty-five minutes he had been there.

I gave him a moment and then rephrased the question. "What do you want God to do for you?"

After another moment of pause, Gary said, "His will, of course."

I said, "Of course," in agreement, "but what do you want?" I could tell that maybe he had not thought that his will could be God's will as well. I admired his heart for God's will to be done in his life, but also wanted him to know that Christ followers can know God's will in situations like this. And furthermore, God wants His will to be known to us. This is how we can have confidence in our prayers being answered.

Quick Lesson on the "Gap"

I spent the next thirty minutes or so sharing with Gary one of my favorite ideas in scripture. I call it the Gap. The Gap is what some people miss when they pray. The Gap is a hole that needs to be filled in between the request we are asking of God and what we pray until the answer comes. I explained it to Gary this way.

In Mark 11:24, there is a very powerful promise from Jesus on Dangerous Prayer:

"I tell you, you can pray for anything, and if you believe that you've received it, it will be yours." Mark 11:24. NLT

Now the Gap is between "You can pray for anything," and "...if you believe that you receive it, it will be yours."

Most people (like me in the past) just start telling God what they want without getting the Gap filled in first.

The Greek word "pray" is also translated "desire" or "*aiteo*" which means "to ask". I told Gary that it is important to first know what it is you want God to do. You must be very clear. So the first step in getting clear on what it is you want from God actually starts with another prayer.

Filling The Gap

"Delight yourself in the LORD and he will give you the desires of your heart." Psalms 37:4 NIV

I said, "Gary, if you pray first by telling God your need, problem, or situation and ask Him what solutions He would recommend, as simple as it may sound, He will answer. Just ask God for the outcome first before you start believing it to happen. Ask God to show you what it looks like, if it were fixed." When we do this, we invite the most powerful being in the universe, our Heavenly Father, to help us, and God will often give us an idea, or a picture of the finished product or situation. I shared Mary and Bill's story as an example.

Mary and Bill

Mary and Bill were at a nasty place in their relationship. It was strained, and they needed help. Mary prayed dangerously and asked God for His advice. Instead of telling God how to fix Bill or their relationship, she simply asked God for the outcome. She asked, "What would our relationship look like, God, if it were fixed? How would it feel?" Within a few days, in her quiet prayer time with God, she got the "idea" of her and Bill laughing hysterically together. As she wrote this in her prayer journal, she saw them as a couple laughing so hard they were holding their stomachs and their cheeks were hurting. She realized that even though this seemed silly, she knew it was from God because the idea came with a peace in her heart.

After seeing the outcome that she believed God gave her, Mary would then lay her head on her pillow at night with that specific picture in her mind and thank God for the answer as she drifted off to sleep. She would even giggle to herself sometimes as the images rolled through her mind. She decided to do this night after night as long as it took until she would experience this specific answer to prayer in her natural life with Bill. This was God's way of helping her develop a sense of certainty that her Prayer was going to be answered. It was God's kind of faith since she knew the idea came from Him.

Cracking the Code

It was about three weeks later that she and Bill were in a coffee shop. While they were there, they were reading humorous greeting cards to one another from a rack in the corner of the shop. The cards were so funny that they started laughing so hard Mary spilled her coffee! Bill was leaning against a wall holding his stomach because it hurt from all his laughter. At that moment it hit Mary that God had answered the very prayer picture He had given her during her quiet time with Him. The same images she went to sleep with every night were actually happening before her very eyes. The gut-busting coffee shop laughter started their relationship in a more life-giving direction. She had cracked the Dangerous Prayer code.

Mary remembered that in Mark 11:24, Jesus was making this God kind of belief a prerequisite to receiving answers to prayer.

"You must believe that you receive your answer when you pray."

Notice it does not say, "After the thing you've desired has come to pass."

I also shared with Gary that some people have mistakenly taken this verse and applied it to praying for other people. Jesus made it very clear that you would have the things that you desired of the Lord, not that they would have the things that you desired of the Lord for them. Other scriptures give promises for praying Dangerous Prayers for others, but this scripture is not one of them. This scripture applies to individuals believing and receiving their own desires.

So, praying back to God specifically what He has given you and agreeing with Him is required when you pray. Scripture tells you the thing you desire "shall come to pass." This may be in an instant, or it may be a longer period of time, but the word "shall" does signify sometime in the future.

I continued to share with Gary that the Lord moves instantly to answer our Dangerous Prayers, but He moves in the spiritual realm first. His breakthrough handiwork is not always immediately seen in our physical realm. By faith, we must be certain that He is answering our prayers before we see any physical evidence. If we stop believing, then we may "cancel the order". We must not let doubt cancel the answer to our prayer!

After we get the specific "prayer picture", we must keep praying by thanking God that He loves us and has already answered our Dangerous Prayer. Then we wait until the picture becomes reality or until the next part of the picture is revealed to us.

Our Best Interest

I told Gary that the next step is very important. Let God create the outcome His way. Matthew 6:33 states that our job is to *"Seek the Kingdom of God and His righteousness and all these things will be added unto us."* Since God has a vantage point that we don't have, it only makes sense to let Him bring about the answer to our prayer His way. He has our best interest in mind. We just need to trust Him to do His best for our good.

Let God decide how to make that specific picture that you are praying for come true. If He chooses to use your weird Uncle Fester to answer your Dangerous Prayers, who cares? Just smile and trust God!

I could tell Gary was soaking it all in like a big sponge. So I asked him again. "What do you want God to do?"

This time, with a lot more confidence, Gary said, "I'll let you know." He realized he didn't have a clear answer because he had not talked to God about filling in the gap for his Dangerous Prayer. We prayed together. As he headed out the door to talk to God again, I could tell something was different.

It was only a couple of days before I got the following very clear email from Gary.

Pastor Alex,

I really appreciate you talking to me today. The insight on my prayer life was awesome. It gave me a proper perspective on how to approach God with my prayers and how to believe in my inner being the answer that God will give me. *I believe God wanted me to learn this so that He could give me more than I imagined. He is so good to me.*

My prayer to Him in this case is for the judge to see the truth of what the intentions of the plaintiff are and to dismiss the case the first day. I am also asking that I would not have to go on the stand, and I want the insurance company to hold me blameless of the costs related. I also want to be exonerated of wrongdoing and any liability. I want for people to see that I am innocent. I believe this in my inner being and am praising the Lord for victory. And I appreciate your prayers.

Sincerely,

Gary

Stress and Worry Washed Away

Gary later told me that prior to his sending me that email, he had prayed dangerously. He had asked God to put the outcome of that answered prayer into his mind so that he could pray to Him "in agreement" with certainty and confidence. He said he had never prayed while lying prostrate on the floor before, but he found himself there while asking God for the picture. He told me as the picture materialized, he had a tremendous peace press against him, one like he had never experienced before. He lay on the floor in this state and just chilled with God. He told me that all the stress and worry about the lawsuit was being drained away by God's companionship.

From Bad to Worse

The trial started on a Monday. Gary wanted the trial to only take one day, but it took three. Gary's main three agreements to pray back to God were to win the case, not have to pay the legal fees and to be exonerated of all charges.

During his first day in court, on the witness stand, Gary was asked a lot of questions that he was limited to either a "yes" or "no" answer. No details could be provided. Gary did exactly as he was instructed. He was so nervous that he was shaking like a leaf while on the stand. Gary had never been through a trial before, and it was quite intimidating, to say the least.

As Lori sat in the courtroom and watched her husband's character be twisted and potentially ruined, she was livid. She said, as she sat watching and listening, "It was driving me crazy." She had not been in any of the meetings with Gary's attorneys so she was wondering why they were allowing this to happen. Finally she sat back and in her heart began to worship and praise the Lord Jesus for the outcome that Gary believed he would get. As she prayed, nothing seemed to happen. As a matter of fact, it seemed to go from bad to worse.

David and Goliath

As I mentioned before, Gary had never experienced a trial before. Unbelievably, he had gotten another subpoena to appear as a witness in another trial in the state supreme court the very next day, which was the second day of his trial. As the higher court took precedence over the lower court, Gary was not present the next day for his own trial. As Lori sat in the courtroom the second day, she was glad that Gary was not present. The plaintiff's battery of attorney's and paralegals were going through what seemed like a mountain of boxes of papers all geared to destroy Gary's character and many years of business ethics. Except for the Dangerous Prayer Lori was holding on to, this bone-crushing experience could have been more than she could bear.

Lori said that after the second day she now understood what David felt when he was going up against that mean and nasty Goliath. She felt very small compared to the Goliath they faced. She worshipped her God even more and thanked Him that He had made a way for Gary to not be there that day.

Ninety Minutes

It was the third and last day of this emotionally draining and painful ordeal. Someone was going to walk out of that courtroom a winner or a loser. Would it be big Goliath or little

David? As this was not a trial with a jury, Gary's attorney's told him that normally, the judge would hear both sides of the case first. After the trial, his verdict could take three to six months. Gary had asked God for a one-day trial. One day turned into three. Now it could take up to six months to know the outcome. Would he lose everything and have to start all over? What a nightmare!

Gary paused and again thought of his time with God the previous week. He remembered lying prostrate on the floor and the peaceful companionship of God. Even though all the details of the trial had not gone exactly as he hoped, he knew God was going to deliver this promise to him. He continued to worship his God in his heart.

As the final details of the trial wrapped up, the judge adjourned the court, saying he said he would give a verdict in one hour. Wow! All the attorneys looked at each other in surprise. Gary looked back at Lori and smiled as she sat praying her Dangerous Prayer, thanking God for the outcome they believed God would provide.

It was actually ninety minutes later when the judge sent the bailiff to round up everyone. With everyone standing, the judge came in to give his verdict.

A Birthday Present

The judge ruled in Gary's favor. Apparently the plaintiff had failed to file some paperwork in regard to his claim seven years earlier and the statute of limitations had run out. This caused the judge to rule in Gary's favor by default. As no substantiated negligence was found on Gary's behalf, his company's insurance company paid all the legal fees. It was not the way Gary hoped to win. He wanted public exoneration. He wanted vindications, and that did not happen.

After all, it was Gary's birthday. The next morning, Gary was praying and thanking God for his victory. It was then that he realized God had indeed answered all three of his prayers, just not in the way Gary expected. God reminded Gary of two important facts. The first was that after the judge had rendered his verdict, someone had been waiting for him as he stepped off the elevator. This person, who Gary did not know and who did not introduce himself, told Gary he had been praying for him during the trial. He had been connected to the plaintiff and realized the plaintiff was not interested in doing the right thing, only financial gain at Gary's expense. He also realized that Gary was an honorable man and was not guilty of any wrong. So during the trial, this stranger began to pray for Gary to win the case even though this person worked for the plaintiff, not Gary.

Gary realized God had publicly exonerated him through this one person! If this was the only person other than his family who knew he was innocent, it was good enough for him. God had done just as He told Gary he would do. He won the trial. He did not have to pay the legal fees. He was exonerated.

Be Specific

I later asked Gary what lesson he would like others to learn through his experience. He looked me straight in the eyes and was very clear and certain. He said he would want people to ask for help early on when pushing through tough times. He shared that he needlessly lugged the weight of that lawsuit around, from the time of being subpoenaed until the day he came to see me a week before court because he was just like most men, too stinking proud to ask for help. (Remember The Invisible Law of Agreement in Chapter 4?)

The last thing he said was to be specific when praying. Find out what is on God's mind about the situation and stay in agreement with Him. Don't pray those "Your will be done" prayers! They always turn out bad. Be specific. Gary said, "If we had not done that, I know our results would have been horrible. Being specific means all the difference."

God had actually answered Gary's prayer over seven years prior when the plaintiff failed to file the proper paperwork on time. As simple as it sounds, when Gary agreed with God on the specifics, God began to move on his behalf. Gary was right. If he had not prayed specifically with God's will, the trial could have turned out very differently. If this sounds strange to you, let me just encourage you to try it and watch God move in your life.

Prayer is the most important thing in a Christian's life. Nothing else is more important. Nothing! The power in prayer is God's power. When you pray, you are inviting God to exercise His power in your life. God wants us to pray about all things. This is why it is important to ask Him to reveal His will to help you to pray like He thinks. Once you have the mind of God on something, then you can pray passionately, confidently and dangerously.

So pray like Gary and Mary.

They asked, "What would our situations look like, God, if it were fixed? How would it feel?" And within a few days, it may be in your quiet prayer time with God or just doing your usual routine, the idea will come to you. And when it does, write it down. Use as many details as possible from gut-busting laughter to the time of day and the place. Whatever God reveals, put it down no matter how silly it may seem. And sense the peace in your heart.

A Gut Wrenching Call

Like Gary, John received an unexpected phone call that left him feeling lost and insecure. One big difference was Gary's pain was coming from complete strangers; not so for John. He was dealing with people that he knew intimately and had loved his whole life. In the next chapter, you'll see how Dangerous Prayers helped him not only get through the fresh pain of an old wound but come out stronger. His strength and love ramped up so high that he became an expression of God's grace to those who had hurt him to the core of his being.

PRAYER SEVEN
The Secret

It's not how many times you fall down; it's how many times you get back up. This type of Dangerous Praying will get you back up stronger than you were when you fell.

Devastating News

On this particular day, John walked into a room full of pastors that he served alongside, broke down and cried like a baby. These pastors who loved him began to embrace his pain and encourage him, even crying with him. Though they poured out their love on him, his broken heart could not receive any of it. Without realizing it, he had let his wounded heart construct a massive stone wall that blocked it all out.

John had gotten some very bad news. Devastating news!

"I can remember feeling like God had ditched me when I received the phone call that my mom and stepdad were getting a divorce. *What? This cannot be happening, again!* It transported back so many feelings of my wrecked childhood, of when my mother and father divorced twenty-five years ago.

I felt so lost and insecure, crushed by the people that I loved the most," John said.

On Paper

One of John's friends said, "You need to cancel all your meetings, stop thinking about work and go spend some time with God." John thought that was the last thing he wanted to do. What he really wanted to do was to bury his emotions with familiar stuff like work or meetings; whatever he could do to short-circuit the pain. He didn't want to deal with the anger, the unforgiveness and the bitterness that was drowning him. Reluctantly, he took his friend's advice, canceled his appointments and just walked away.

After talking to his wife, he booked a hotel room an hour or so away. As he halfheartedly drove to the hotel he thought, *What good is it going to do for me to just sit in a hotel room by myself spending time with God? How is that going to take this pain away?* Arriving at his room, he felt lost with no idea what to do. He decided to just pour out his feelings to God on paper.

I recently found out my stepfather has been having an affair. My heart is so broken for my mom and the rest of our family. I am so disappointed by someone I admired and looked up to. He has been a father figure to me for over twenty years. I feel so resentful towards him now. I'm disappointed in him. I'm angry! Most of all, I feel sorry for him. I know my stepfather is not living life with the Lord and honestly, I'm worried for his life. I have always had this expectation in my heart for him to make things right with God and that still hasn't happened.

John could not understand why his stepfather did not run to God, especially in this desperate time. As much as he resented him, at the moment, he wanted God to help him. As ticked off as he was at his actions, he still wanted him to be okay. Darn it, he loved his stepfather so much.

Too Many Feelings

Too many feelings surged through John to process. His emotional cup was flooded with all the wrong things. What he needed was Holy Spirit to come in and pull the plug on his heart. He needed to remember that he was in an emotional and spiritual freefall.

The verse in Romans 8:28 had been blaring in John's head over and over, *"All things work together for the good of them who love God and are called for His purpose."* At the time, he didn't know how God could possibly make this whole mess work together for good. He knew God had a 50,000-foot view of things that John couldn't see.

Makes No Sense

After pouring out his heart to God, the most natural thing his soul wanted to do was to worship, even though his heart was broken, and the pain was still excruciating. Looking back on it later, John said that it almost didn't even make sense to him to do that. Why would he want to worship when the world would have told him to vent, to gossip, to fight or just do something to please his flesh?

But instead, John put on worship music and began to cry out his love for his Daddy in heaven. As he did this, such peace and healing began to come over him that he wrote these words and began to sing out a song that was rising up in his heart.

How deep is the Father's love for us. I keep finding myself fall.

He embraces my sorrow with His loving arms. And turns it into everlasting joy.

John was amazed at the presence of God. He marveled as to how he could go from such a dark, depressed place to being full of joy. His world had just been shattered, yet he was stress free and full of peace and hope. Was he burying the pain deep down inside, where it would only resurface later? What was happening? Was he losing touch with reality because of the pain? Was he going insane?

Actually, it was just the opposite. You see, John found out that something very special happens when your Dangerous Prayer becomes worship. As he poured out his heart, the only thing he wanted to do was worship God. It was the natural next step. It was really the only thing that did make sense. He couldn't fight back the feeling; he had to let God know how he felt about Him in that moment. He had to give God worth and worship.

In the Old Testament, King David prayed for God to create in him a clean heart. In the NIV, Psalm 51, he said this in verse 6, *"Surely you desire truth in the inner parts."* John had come to God with the excruciatingly painful truth. It was exactly what God wanted him to do. While God did not cause the pain, John was certain He would use it. Heal it.

God Encounter

"So let us come boldly to the throne of our gracious God. There we will receive mercy, and we will find grace to help us when we need it most." Hebrews 4:16 NLT

The next day John wrote in his journal:

I felt Your embrace helping me through this burden I'm carrying. I must lay it down at the foot of the cross. My emotions can't control me, and now I feel I have better understanding of how to guard my heart from that happening. I am spirit first made in the image of my Heavenly Father. My soul is the one out of line. I say to you, soul, be quiet and be still! Spirit, I speak to you also and tell you to rise up! I give you permission to rise up and control my life. You will do a much better job than I will at trying to control it and keep things in order.

As John dangerously prayed for help, God took his burden. God had traded with him. For John's worship, God gave relief and it never came back. John was totally relieved. He knew, at that moment, that his disappointing childhood past would not determine his future; God's love would!

As he humbled himself at God's feet in worship, Holy Spirit melted his heart. He gave John a fresh anointing. Holy Spirit became his confidence, strength and coach. He was all John needed.

Now, since he was basking in his Heavenly Father's love and he was empowered to give it away, he could now comfort his mom and extended family and help them work through the mess. Amazingly, he was even able to help his stepdad.

From that point forward, his words became encouraging and life giving in what seemed to be a dead situation. The outcome was not his responsibility. He was only responsible for his heart's response and for his Dangerous Prayer. He now could choose to forgive and forget. He left the judging up to God. His only vow would be love. God took John's pain away and changed his heart.

He found himself worshipping again after writing in his journal. He remembers hearing these words come from his mouth. They were lyrics from a Hillsong tune called *Love Like Fire*:

Let Your love take me deeper
Draw me closer to where You are
All I want is more of You
When You call I will follow
At the cross I surrender all
Jesus, I belong to You.

Can I Really Do This?

When Dangerous Prayers and worship meet, you begin to realize the source of your strength. Like in Chapter One, the identity of who you really are rises in God's presence. It's where you find direction and realize that you are in God's family and that nothing can separate you from His love.

In Matthew 6:9-13, The Lord's Prayer, begins and ends with worship. *"Our Father in heaven, hallowed be Your name...for Yours is the kingdom, and the power, and the glory, forever, Amen."*

Also, Psalm 29:2 tells us to give unto the Lord the glory due His name. Can you have prayer and no worship? You can, but when you add authentic worship, it changes everything.

It was John's last day at the hotel. He was about to pack up, check out, and head back to the real world. Part of him didn't want to leave because of his heavenly experience with God.

This was his last journal entry.

Leaving

This is my last moment here and I can truly say, God, I've learned a lot. But learning and applying are on opposite ends of a bridge. As I'm about to grab my bag to go check out, I feel a sense of worry. Can I do this? Can I continue to make You my priority all the time? My Dangerous Prayer is YES, with Your help, Holy Spirit! By Your power and Your might! I know I am weak but with You living in me, I leave with faith that says, "YES I can do this!" Yes, I will continue to worship You and put You first. I love You Jesus. I love You Holy Spirit. I love you Father!

Your Son, John

So John worshipped as he dangerously prayed for the endurance, the strength, the power and the boldness to apply everything he had learned. He knew that God had given him the power to blow away the enemy of his soul and to love the unlovable.

Dangerous Prayer and Praise

J.R.R. Tolkien was right when he said, "All that is gold does not glitter; not all those who wander are lost." As John dangerously prayed to God, his words turned from pain to praise. God filled his mouth with gold, with value, and with praise and worship that he gave back to God. Even though he wandered, he was never lost. His Daddy in Heaven was always there.

When Dangerous Prayers of praise flow out of our hearts and mouth, powerful things happen. Consider adding praise and worship to your Dangerous Prayer time. Over time, it will become an indispensable part of your time with God. And when you go through dark times, the power of praise and worship for your Father in Heaven will fill you with strength that at the time, like John said, may not make sense, but it's God's gift to you. You are His child, and He's crazy about you.

"You will keep in perfect peace all who trust in you, all whose thoughts are fixed on you!" Isaiah 26:3 NLT

Friday the 13th

It was Friday the 13th, and Anne will always love that day! That was the day her Daddy in Heaven did an amazing thing for her. He gave her the answer to a Dangerous Prayer that she had prayed four years before. But in the next chapter you will see that it cost Anne more than most are willing to pay to see their Dangerous Prayers come true.

PRAYER EIGHT
Never, Never, Never Give Up

Wait...don't pray until you are really ready. Then, saw the limb off, burn the ships, cut the ropes, let go of everything that can save you...and you will see the hand of God.

Before you read this, understand this is not just Anne's story about her dream house named Charlotte. It's Anne's story of bulldog-persistent, childlike faith. The kind of persistent faith that makes your friends look at you like you are crazy. You-have-lost-your-mind, what-is-wrong-with-that-girl? kind of crazy. But Anne simply believed that her Father in Heaven told her the truth. He was giving her something, and she believed Him.

Simply Believe

In 2008, Anne's family had just moved to Manatee County in Florida. Anne didn't know the area well. So she would go online looking at houses for sale. One day while surfing the usual prospects of houses for sale on the web, she totally fell in love with this one particular house.

Unfortunately, it was way out of her price range. I mean way out of it. She downloaded all of the pictures of that house and stored them on her computer as a "vision book" just so she could keep it in mind for the house that she would one day own.

Anne kept those pictures for almost three years before she resigned herself that it was just a fact of life that she would just have to let go of that house and be content with what she could afford. God had always provided what she needed, so she was going to be thankful with whatever house He decided was best for her family. But in her heart she still dreamed of that house.

Four years later, she and her husband Stan had finally decided that they were going to be staying in the area permanently. Anne was from the beautiful hills of Virginia, so Florida was quite different from her home state, but they started house hunting. She knew they wanted to live out in the country as much as possible. One Sunday afternoon, as she and Stan were driving, he received a call and needed to write something down.

He turned onto the only side street they could quickly find and pulled over. *What a nice neighborhood*, Anne thought to herself. Anne had no idea there was a community like that out in the country. As her husband was talking and writing, she looked up at the street sign. Her jaw dropped. She realized it was the same street on which her dream house she had found on the Internet four years earlier had been located. No way!

No One Wanted Her...Except Me!

"I got chills," Anne said. She was so excited she could barely keep herself from interrupting Stan while he was on the phone. Her look at Stan said, *Get off the phone...now!* She was thinking that she was finally going to be able to see it in person and get closure. She thought, *I know, I know! It's just a house, but...I just loved it.* So after Stan was off the phone, they slowly drove down the road and looked at all the houses trying to find *her.* As they rounded a corner, Anne saw her. She loved her even more in person.

Then she saw *it.* The *For Sale* sign at the end of the driveway. Could it be? She was for sale again? Wait! Then they noticed how her yard was overgrown and there was a sticker in the window. They pulled into the driveway and walked to the front door. It was BANK OWNED!

"No one wanted her. No one except me!" Anne said.

They found out from the listing agent the house had just entered the auction process. They swallowed hard. Were they too late? For some reason, the listing agent wouldn't help them with the bank's information. They were hoping they could catch it and make an offer. Not only did the agent refuse to help them, but was downright rude! The house was going to auction.

Well, that was that. Anne was heartbroken and confused. She didn't understand why God would bring her to this house four years later, only to dangle it in front of her and then say, "Never mind you can't have it." What was going on here?

Anne's daughter Janie heard her mom's confusion and said, "Mom, God doesn't work that way. He doesn't tease! Why would He bring you to Charlotte (Anne's personal name for the house) and then just take her right back? He wouldn't. If He wants you to have her, then you will!"

It was then that God started to whisper to Anne, *Trust me. Have childlike faith.* It was one of those *Aha!* moments. She heard Him loud and clear. She decided immediately she was going to be like her daughter, and so she would bid on the house.

Thank You, Father

Stan had been in one of my small groups, and I had taught them to listen to our Father in Heaven about Dangerous Prayers and anointing oil. Stan would go home every night after our small group would finish and sometimes after midnight would re-teach the lessons to Anne. She was so excited to learn.

So now she and Stan decided to walk the perimeter of the property, anoint it with oil and pray. They anointed every entrance and every exit. They then wrote, *Thank you, Lord, for our new home* on a 3x5 card and dated it. They slipped the card under the carpet in one of the closets. If their Father in Heaven wanted to give them this house, then they were by all means going to have it! Anne wanted Him to know that she understood this was a story of faith, and she was going to trust Him and not give up, which is a key essential part of a Dangerous Prayer.

They quickly set a meeting with their realtor and mortgage agent to discuss the auction process and how to bid. That afternoon, before she and her husband left for the meeting, Anne sensed the Lord telling her that they didn't need to bid. She knew it sounded crazy. How else would they get the house? However, Anne was practicing her persistent childlike faith in hearing and following her Heavenly Father. He knew best! She told her husband that they should not bid. Stan looked at her at first like she was a total nut! She said she knew how she must have sounded but what could she do? Her Father in Heaven said, "Don't bid," so they should not bid.

They went to the appointment, and as they sat down with their agent and mortgage broker, Anne could tell from their faces something was wrong. They started with "Anne, we know how much you have your heart set on this house, but..."

They basically said it was a horrible and financially dangerous idea to try to bid on that house. This kind of bidding was set up for investors, not for the average homebuyer. They went on to say that she and Stan could potentially lose thousands and thousands of dollars if they made one wrong move in the very delicate process.

Anne knew they were serious, but she just had to laugh! She told them they had already decided not to bid. She told them it was their house because their Father in Heaven was giving it to them. They had prayed and anointed it and had accepted this house as His gift. The rest was His problem to work out. So Anne and Stan went home, leaving the agent and mortgage broker scratching their heads. Anne just knew they must have thought, *These people must be nuts.*

The auction was nine days later. "Now, I admit, I did watch it. I had to see what would happen," said Anne. For some strange reason no one bid on the house. Not a single investor!

Then the house had to be sent back to the real estate company for another try at selling it. Three days later, a friend at the title company forwarded an email to Anne that said, *This property is actively on the market, is a bank-owned foreclosure and is vacant. If your friends would like to look at it, let me know. We can get them in as soon as possible.*

Mustard Seed

"Trust is the fruit of a relationship in which you know you are loved."~Wm. Paul Young, *The Shack*

"It was then that I felt that I needed to stand on Matthew 17:20, the mustard seed verse," Anne said. She even ordered a necklace with a key and a mustard seed inside the key and wore it every day. Her faith was as big as that mustard seed! So she just sat back and watched as God kept moving.

She told as many people as she could about the house. It's funny how much you learn about people when you are dealing with matters of faith. Anne quickly learned who had it and who didn't. Who actually believed and who just thought she was as nutty as a fruitcake.

However, she had many friends that didn't even question the situation. They agreed that if God said it was to happen, they would continue dangerously praying in agreement right along with her. The house went through another auction process for five days and no one purchased it.

Stan and Anne's mortgage loan commitment wouldn't allow them to buy the house in its current need of repairs, so Anne assumed someone had to purchase it to first make repairs, then they could buy it. They watched the house go through two more auctions and still no buyers.

It was after that that they found the weed. You read it right—a weed. She and Stan made routine visits to the house to make sure no one was vandalizing it since it had been empty for so long. On a visit, Anne walked into the living room, and there it was.

A stinking weed was growing in the corner of the living room! Something about that weed hit Anne in a bad way. It was like some kind of poison. She said, "It literally felt like a knife in my heart." A weed in the corner of a room inside the house! What else could there be? Had she been wrong all this time? Was God telling her that she was letting this house become a weed in her own life? Now she was really confused.

They Walked Away

It was at this time they decided to just walk away from the house. As much as it hurt, they began to look at other houses. They found one they liked and made an offer. A friend said, "I know this is your home. God brought you through all of that to have THIS house." Anne remembers looking at her, sort of detached. "My husband and kids loved the house, but I felt nothing," she said.

She believed that God had said she was to have Charlotte. They even anointed Charlotte. Where did she go wrong? Anne had never felt so sure about anything in her entire life as she did about getting that home! Everything in her being felt like that was her house.

She later told a dear friend who was a pastor's wife about it. She said, "I was doing the right thing. I had to look at other houses so when we got Charlotte, we would know it was from God." She already knew that, but there she was buying a different house. This was ridiculous. On paper, the new house had everything her family wanted. The problem was, Anne didn't feel it in her heart. She prayed that God would close the door if they weren't supposed to have the house.

They got a call two days later about the house they made an offer on. The owner took a different offer. What? They took a full price offer from friends of theirs. *Friends? Really? How does that work?* Even though it was perfectly legal, the realtor said he had never seen anything like it in his entire career. Anne was unfazed. She knew it wasn't the one God had for them.

Anne continued to check on Charlotte's status online every day just to see if there had been any changes. Then all of a sudden, it disappeared. Poof! Just like that, the house had vanished from the listings. It was no longer up for auction. What a circus of events. What was going on?

How About My Kidneys too?

However, the very next day Anne checked on the house again. It was back. No explanations; it was there, it was gone, now it's back. What the heck was going on? There was no mention of the word *auction* in the listing. It looked like it was just up for sale.

What? Anne snatched up her phone and called her realtor immediately. She and Stan must have set a record for how fast an offer was submitted that day.

The next day the listing agent said the bank would not accept the offer unless they were pre-approved by a specific mortgage lender. That sounded a little fishy. Anne and Stan had already been approved through their chosen mortgage company. Anne prayed, "Okay, Lord, I will jump through any hoops they throw our way." It seemed they were asking for everything but their kidneys.

While waiting for the new pre-approval, they got a call that the offer had been accepted. They were finally, officially, in a contract with the bank!

A call from the mortgage company demanded that they would still need additional special approval from the underwriting department. Three very long days later, the VP of underwriting came back and rendered them approved.

Anne and Stan felt like they had been in a spiritual tornado since the first time they laid eyes on that house. Even though they held onto their bulldog-persistent faith, they were whipped. They were flat-out tired spiritually, physically and emotionally. That weekend, Anne told me that she felt like they were a little half crazed after being on the front lines of battle for months. But they finally figured it out, and now Anne and Stan knew how to build faith. It comes through listening to God's voice, obeying God's voice and, oh yeah, not quitting. They wished there had been an easier way, but all it took was a mustard seed, stick-to-it kind of faith. Good thing, because that was all Anne and Stan had.

Friday the 13th

Anne said, "It was Friday the 13th. I will always love that day! That was the day my Father in Heaven did an amazing thing for me. He gave me my house, Charlotte!" The house she had loved for four long years and had been believing for with a wild, childlike, persistent faith was finally hers! Their persistent Dangerous Prayers had worked. On that day Anne said she felt like she could cry for days.

She knew all along it was going to happen but to actually hold the keys to Charlotte in her hand was so humbling. God's love for her was overwhelming. She knew she would never be the same and neither would her faith. Childlike persistent faith and Dangerous Prayer—I guess that was God's plan all along, wasn't it? It's a winning combination, but it's not for the faint of heart or quitters.

Anne

Anne and her husband Stan's trust in God grew like crazy. I mean it became gargantuan size. They realized He is very much interested in their everyday needs and wants to throw down and help out when they believe.

Anne's story should encourage you if you are struggling with your faith. Never give up! If God says He will do it, don't try to figure it out for Him. Just sit back and let Him do it for you. At times, it won't make sense to you, and it may even be very scary. But He will come through for you. You could never plan it any better.

If you are a Christ-follower, you are not of this world, but of His world. You are just a visitor here. You are not completely bound by all the rules of this world. You are a supernatural being and should live that way. You are a son or a daughter of God. If He cares so much about a house, imagine how much He cares about your finances, job, health, etc.

Bulldog-Like Faith

"Never, never, never give up." ~ Winston Churchill

Persistent faith is a critical piece in getting your Dangerous Prayers answered. Sometimes your faith can get a little scraped up and bruised when you go through pain and hardships. Sometimes the bitter pills of life can cause you to want to stop believing. But you must stay innocent and not judge God about his method of working things out for you. If, like Anne, you decide in your heart to hang in there with bulldog determination, you will see God answer your Dangerous Prayers. She decided that God had a good heart and that He wanted to give her a house. Anne did not know how or exactly when, but she knew that God would help her and He did.

From Weed to Idol

Like the weed that had sprung up in Anne's dream home became a distraction from what God had promised her, Linda had a weed of a different sort in her life. Linda's "weed" grew up. It became an "idol", a really mean and nasty one; one that millions of Americans still worship today with their blood, sweat, tears and millions of dollars. And in the next chapter you will see how if it weren't for Linda's Dangerous Prayer, that monster could have stopped her for good.

PRAYER NINE
Focused

A 150-watt light bulb can light up a room, but a 150-watt focused laser beam can cut through steel. Dangerous Prayers get laser-like power from one focus.

Wandering

Sometimes we all just flat out get lost, clueless even, and the easiest way to get into trouble is to stay lost, whether it is lost on a trip, lost in finances or lost in relationships. When you are lost, you wander and don't know how to find your way. You may make a bad turn and travel in a direction that could lead to great pain and even death, but remember it's not the trip, the finances or the relationship that's to blame.

"Where there is no vision the people perish…" Proverbs 29:18 KJV

It's the "wandering" that can hurt you. In Proverbs 29:18, part of the definition of the word perish is "to wander aimlessly". When you don't put a purpose and vision to your money, your relationship, and yes, even your health, "idols" can. And when "idols" become your focus, over time you may find yourselves in really painful situations like my friend, Linda.

"Legs" Day

In August 2009, early one morning, Linda was going to the gym to work out with her workout buddy, Mia. Linda made it to the gym first, so she decided to hit the treadmill until Mia arrived. Linda loved running! She had been a runner all her life. She decided to add weights into her workout to get into the best shape she could.

Over time, working out became her personal obsession. Never missing a workout, six days a week, exercising was more important to Linda than anything else. She also loved working out with Mia, because Mia enjoyed killer workouts as much as she did. Linda's workouts led her to competing in fitness competitions. She loved all the attention.

When Mia arrived, they decided it was "legs" day. They did their regular warm-ups, then squats. For this workout, Linda put more weight on the machine than ever before. No pain, no gain! She was determined to keep up with Mia! Even though it already felt very heavy, she was very competitive and determined to keep up.

Linda said, "As I was doing the last squat in my set, something abnormal happened." She had dropped down a little farther than she ever had before, but when she came back up, something didn't feel right in her lower back, something inside. She said that she should have stopped then, but she continued to push through the workout.

As she moved to the leg machine, she could tell something felt out of whack. She didn't listen to her body and kept going. After completing her leg routine, she hit the treadmill for a final thirty minutes. As she ran, she felt it. A pain started shooting down her right leg. Again, she just ignored it and kept running. No pain, no gain, right? She wasn't going to let a little pain get in the way of her getting into shape and physically looking good. After her run, she stretched, cooled down, and headed home.

Working Through the Pain

On the way home, Linda noticed the shooting pain was still there, but it wasn't sharp enough to keep her from her workouts. "It was more annoying than anything else," Linda said. Several times the following week, she felt the pain creep down her lower back and target her leg, and it was not letting go. The pain started growing. It now started hassling her when she would do simple things, like walking. The only relief she felt was when she was sitting down.

The next Wednesday she went to the gym, again hoping to push through the pain. This time she was by herself so she ran on the treadmill instead of working with weights. When she tried to run, the pain became brutally excruciating, and she had to stop cold. She helplessly limped out of the gym to her car. Linda didn't realize it at the time but this would be the first day of a long recovery.

"You Will Never Run Again."

Linda went to bed every night and woke up each morning with the same vicious pain, day after day. Walking became almost unbearable. There were many days when she had to leave work early as the gripping pain was too excruciating to bear. Finally, Linda decided it was time to get some help.

She paid a visit to the chiropractor and then to a physical therapist. Finding no relief, she tried an acupuncturist. Finally, with a lot of prodding from her family and friends, she went to her medical doctor. After seeing the terrible pain she was in, the doctor told her she needed to have an MRI immediately so she could fully diagnose the problem. The doctor gave Linda prescriptions for muscle relaxants and pain and scheduled an MRI for the next week. Linda took both medications looking for some relief, but neither one fazed her as she continued to endure the agony when she walked.

The day finally came for the MRI. It was uncomfortable and a little scary, but Linda didn't care. By this time, all she wanted was the pain to go away. When the results from the MRI came back, her doctor told her that she had a herniated disc, which was irritating her sciatic nerve. All Linda knew is it felt like white hot coals were burning her alive every time she moved. The doctor recommended pain management therapy, which meant they would give Linda shots in her back with long needles to relieve the pain. After she made the appointment, she cancelled it two days later. Even in her pain, God began speaking to her. Linda said, "I knew in my spirit that He was not in favor of that therapy. I trusted in Him, and knew He would take care of me and answer my Dangerous Prayer to be pain free."

After she cancelled the pain management therapy, daily she prayed dangerously for God to take the pain away. She began physical therapy and decompression therapy, thinking God would work through the physical therapist to help her. It only gave her temporary relief, but then the pain would come back with a vengeance. She was told by another physical therapist that she would probably need surgery and would never run again. "I knew God didn't want that for me," Linda said.

Dangerous Prayer of Faith

It had been almost a month since the pain attacked Linda, and she knew she had a decision to make. Linda again had asked many of her friends and relatives for advice.

Finally, one day she talked with a friend who told her, "Go see Pastor Alex and have him pray for you."

Linda said, "I felt a peace in my spirit and knew that was what I needed to do. That next Sunday, I was hoping I would see him. I did, and at the end of the church service, I asked him to pray for me. Of course he said he would and asked another woman to join us in the prayer. Before he started praying, he asked what I wanted prayer for, and I told him about the pain in my back. He asked if I was a believer in what Jesus did for us on the cross and I said I was. He said that Jesus' body was broken so that ours does not have to be broken.

"He then prayed that the Holy Spirit would fill me from the top of my head to the tips of my toes. As he was praying, I could feel a warmness enter my body. I actually felt it run from the top of my head to the tips of my toes as I lifted my hands. Pastor Alex continued asking for healing for me during the prayer. Afterwards, he explained to me that since we had asked for healing, I should thank our Heavenly Father for answering that prayer. That is exactly what I did."

Linda knew she had faith that God would heal her but her mind kept wondering, *when?* One week went by, then two weeks, then a third, and still, no relief. By this time, it was a week before Christmas. She had made plans to go to Kansas to spend Christmas with her family. She was honestly not sure she would be able to make the trip. She didn't think she could handle the walk through the airport because she was still in an incredible amount of pain. Fortunately for Linda, her daughter was there to help her when she arrived at the airport. They rode the special carts in the airport to get from terminal to terminal. What a sight. Linda had been a runner and now was riding a cart to get around. What had brought her to this sad state? She had lost her focus.

I once heard that fog is nothing but confused light. The problem with fog is it makes everything look alike from a distance. No focus, only confusion. Linda was not focused on the source of her life's power, but that was about to change and for the better.

Be Still and Know that I Am God

Before she left for the trip, she said the Lord was telling her it was time for her to urgently put everything aside, to be still and to immerse herself in a flood of Bible reading; listening to God as he spoke to her from the pages. It was time to dangerously pray and focus on the source of all life and light, Jesus Christ. She immediately decided to be at God's beck and call and to journal everything that happened.

"God longs for you to discover the life He created you to live." ~Rick Warren, *The Purpose Driven Life*

On her flight to Kansas City, she turned to the first page in her journal and wrote the date, Dec. 21, 2009. Her entry read:

On the airplane to K.C: Looking forward to reading my Bible and studying God's word. Speak to me, Lord! My back is hurting so bad again today. Lord, I know you want me to slow down and be still, but when will you take this miserable pain away from me? Will I ever run again?

Then she read 2 Corinthians 12:9 ESV, which says, *"My grace is sufficient for you, for my power is made perfect in weakness."*

She began to pray dangerously as she focused on God's grace for her.

"I hear You, Lord. I am listening, I'll do my best to be still, to study and saturate myself in Your promises and be prepared for what You have for me. I love You and thank You for healing me!"

She had planned on spending ten fun-filled days in Kansas with her family. Those plans got radically changed. While she and her daughter were there, God sent a beautiful snowstorm that kept her locked away inside her parents' farmhouse for five of those ten days—more Dangerous Prayer focus time. Her next journal entry was dated Dec. 22, 2009:

Thank You, Lord, for this most beautiful winter day in Kansas. Thank You for bringing me here safely to enjoy time with my family and my friends. Thank You for the peace you have given me. As I sit in this chair with this pain, financial instability and other worldly problems, Your peace sets me free. You have saved me by sending Your son who gives me hope. Romans 5:3-5: My suffering is producing perseverance, character and hope. Thank you, Jesus. God has poured out His love into our hearts by the Holy Spirit whom He has given to us. Your Grace is still sufficient for me. I love you!

Journal Entry Dec. 26, 2009:

I am reading in Matthew about all of the amazing and wonderful miracles You performed. What awesome things You did while here on earth! I believe that You are bringing about an awesome healing in me! My back and legs are feeling no pain today! I can tell Your healing hand is working in me. Thank You! Thank You so much, Jesus! I love you!!

Her final entry from that trip, Dec. 31, 2009:

Thank You, Dear Lord, for another year! It was a year of schooling for me as I reflect back. Besides all the lessons I had to learn, I turned back to You to attend to me. I'm so excited about the relationship we have now! Thank You!

You have always been there for me even when I was unaware of Your tender attention. I'm so happy to be where I am right now working for You! Living my every moment for You! Please continue to heal my spirit and my physical body. Lord, I can feel the pain letting go of my body. Help me to continue to be still and listen to You. Thank You for healing me! I love YOU!!

No More Idols

From that day on, God forged ahead to heal Linda's back. Even though it didn't make a lot of sense, she was obedient and dangerously focused Him as her only source of healing. She stood up and made the decision to no longer let the workouts, alcohol or friends be her idols. Jesus became the only idol in her life and she would live for Him from then on. This was the assignment she believed God wanted her to own. Even though He did not cause it to happen, Linda took a severe back injury as motivation to help her fully focus on where God wanted her and where He was taking her. Linda said, "I thank Him every day for what He did for me through this back injury and how He miraculously healed me." Linda's

Dangerous Prayer focus allowed God to heal her without medicines or therapy.

On May 22, she bought her first running shoes since her back injury. She put those babies on and out the door she went. So on that day she was able to blow through two miles without any pain. Bam! She is now in better physical shape than she was before her injury. She has no pain and is able to jog for about five miles.

No more confused light for Linda. Linda is crystal clear on what is different now. "Working out is not my idol. Yes, I still love to run! I now only run and do my workouts—without weights—after I have read my Father's Word and spent time with Him for the day."

Linda's primary focus is her relationship with her Heavenly Father. She keeps her eyes peeled daily for what He wants her to do for Him to better the world we live in. She praises God for her healing and all of the blessings He showers on her each and every day! Linda now loves to say, "I love You, my Father! Your amazing love has set me free. Thank You Lord for always answering my Dangerous Prayers."

"It's in Christ that we find out who we are and what we are living for. Long before we first heard of Christ...He had His eye on us, had designs on us for glorious living, part of

the overall purpose He is working out in everything and everyone." Ephesians 1:11 MSG

No More Wandering

Dangerous Prayer is focused. It's looking in only one direction for all of your life's needs. Linda was confused and looking at idols. Fitness was her passion and what gave her satisfaction from how it made her look to how it made her feel. However, when the focus is in the direction of a "dead idol" that has no real power, then all that's left is disappointment and pain. When Linda's focus became Jesus, not only did she get her Dangerous Prayer for healing answered, she was also blessed to be able to run again. Bonus! She hadn't even thought of that. But Jesus did.

Sometimes when we pray and get what we want, we can mistake "it" for all of God's answers to our Dangerous Prayers. But God always answers our Dangerous Prayers with peace first, then the "thing" we ask for happens. It's not the other way around. In the next chapter, my friend Angela learned that when we have peace, even if it's a "God whisper", that's all we really need to know our Dangerous Prayers are being answered.

PRAYER TEN
God Whispers

The peace of God stands guard over you like a commando. Learning to recognize it can save the lives of those you love.

My Gang

When I was in the fourth grade at Waccamaw School in Ash, North Carolina, I remember having a gang. Yes, I had a small posse. We would hang out on the playground and plan our gutsy attacks on our rival gang. Now before your mind goes places that it shouldn't, let me explain. I was ten years old, and this was make-believe.

At any rate, we had our own secret handshake, a special code of conduct and "whispers". Whispers were cool because in a few coded words we could communicate in each other's ear vital strategic information about our "rock 'em, sock 'em" maneuvers against our enemies. This was pretty advanced stuff for fourth graders. On the playground, our ten-year-old minds were ablaze with codes and secrets that could only be whispered to another blood brother in the gang. We even used thumbtacks to pierce our thumbs and rub them together to become "true" blood brothers and show our allegiance to the gang. If my own kids had come home and told me they did this, I would have fainted. Times have changed.

Looking back at those days, I now see how intimate and special "whispers" were as a form of communication. Whispers were only to be shared by blood brothers who had each other's backs. Christ followers have the same type of communication available to them with God through Dangerous Prayers; God whispers to us. In his book, *The Spiritual Man*, Watchman Nee says God communicates through Holy Spirit to our spirit. This communication is called *Spiritual Intuition* or better yet, my definition, *whispers*. Our spirit then pushes it to us through a *knowing*. Knowing is not like human knowledge of facts and information. It's more like a feeling you get about something but can't explain it. Nee explains that it's more of a *sense*.

"After the earthquake came a fire, but the LORD was not in the fire. And after the fire came a gentle whisper." 1 Kings 19:12 NIV

I remember hearing Tim Sanders, former Chief Solutions Officer for Yahoo, explain it this way. He had been delayed getting to a meeting that was to be held in the Twin Towers in New York City the morning of 9/11. He obviously was spared the tragedy, but Tim's wife who was back in California could not communicate with him so she had no way of knowing whether he was dead or alive. He said it was days before they could talk so he could not tell her that he was alive and well. Tim's wife had a great support group from her church. As they would try to console her over the possibility of Tim's death, she said she knew he was alive, even though she could not talk to him and verify it. She could *sense* in her spirit that he was well.

Spiritual intuition is God's way of whispering personal and sometimes urgent information to us. These whispers, if listened to by Christ followers, can give us great direction and peace in our lives. Whispers are not only life-giving, but can be life directing as well as they were for Jim and Angela.

Jim and Angela are authentic Christ followers. They are the real deal. They are dedicated to Christ, but they are very transparent and real about their life with Him. One of my favorite things to do is to hang out at the Information Desk at our church before and after services talking to new visitors. Angela, who serves there faithfully, and I have talked for years. One weekend she shared some of her life story. She told me how God had guided her and Jim over the years through "God Whispers". I thought, hmm...whispers...why does that sound familiar?

Angela's First Eighteen Years

In the mid 90's, Angela was a believer but not a Christ-follower. At the time, she would have disagreed with that statement, but now, in hindsight, she realizes it was true. She was raised in the Presbyterian Church, a faithful attendee every Sunday with her family. Her mother led her and her three siblings in a daily devotion every morning after breakfast before they each headed out the front door for school and work. Angela was involved in the youth group at her church as well as at another local church where more of her peeps hung out. Yes, she was a believer.

When she was fourteen, Angela and her sister, Ally, were in a life-threatening accident. The doctors told her mom that Ally was bleeding internally. They couldn't figure out where the bleeding was coming from or how to stop it. They wanted to do exploratory surgery to get some answers.

At about the same time, a prayer vigil began at Angela's church for her sister's healing. A few hours later, the doctors told Angela's mom that out of the blue, the bleeding had stopped. The doctors were perplexed.

Angela's first eighteen years were spent with full exposure to God. She was even given a front row seat to a healing miracle when she was just fourteen. Yet, she went to college without truly knowing the grace and love of God that would lead to her "God Whispers".

Real Life

Angela met her husband during college and they married in 1994. She and Jim decided to live in the college town where they met. It was a beautiful, small southern town that tripled in size during home football games. They loved the community, the tailgating, visiting with friends and family. At that point, life was intoxicatingly perfect.

After a few years into their marriage, they began to realize that the fall months were invigorating but the rest of the year was, well, kind of lousy. Angela was teaching kindergarten in the school of her dreams and Jim was working for a drywall company while finishing school. As they settled into the culture of real life versus college life, they also began to notice general attitudes and opinions of locals they didn't enjoy. According to Angela, though racial issues weren't what they were in the 60's, there were still underlying currents that flowed in both directions. Some days the town felt smaller and smaller.

One thing Jim taught Angela about herself is how crazy she was about the beach. She loved the way the sand felt on her feet, the smell of the ocean and the feeling of salt water drying on her skin. Around 1995, she and Jim began to feel the trap of being land locked and decided they wanted to move to the coast. Being a teacher, Angela could move almost anywhere and find a job. And since Jim wasn't really locked into a career yet, their search for the perfect beachside community became based upon what he could do. He found an opportunity to be a hot shot with the marine patrol boys of the state wildlife and fisheries department near a sleepy little town close to one of their favorite beach spots. They decided this had to be their perfect piece of heaven because both of them loved the beach and could both get work.

Learning To Hear The Whispers

Angela helped Jim find this job by searching online which was a brand spanking new thing at the time. They were sure this had to be the right move because they were both rocking in the possibilities. However, deep inside, Angela felt this gnawing in her soul, this quiet whisper that was telling her, *Not yet.*

She didn't tell Jim because she dismissed it as part of her personality. In some ways, Angela didn't like change and as much as she was would love to leave her college town, she wasn't desperate by any means. Jim, on the other hand, was very excited about the road ahead and Angela didn't want to squash his dreams. She wanted to be the supportive wife, rolling with what life was bringing her. After all, this had been a joint decision even if she had itty-bitty doubts.

With laser-like focus, Jim pursued the marine patrol position. For some odd reason, the job didn't work out and as a result, they stayed put. Angela was disappointed and relieved at the same time. She was a mixed bag of emotions. Ironically, a short time later, Jim told her he had not felt totally settled with the decision either.

Hired On The Spot

A few years later, in February of 2000, Angela and Jim were visiting their favorite beach town with their daughter Ashley, who was almost three, and Jim's folks. Angela remembers everything about being on the beach that day. It was chilly, but the sky was a beautiful blue and the clouds were big and puffy. Ashley had on a pink and white nylon-jogging suit with a white turtleneck, a white knit hat with a pom-pom on top and her Keds. As Angela was watching Ashley play on the beach, she experienced a very powerful sense of peace. She thought, *we should be by the water, not land locked in a town where the closest water is four hours away.*

She turned to Jim that day on the beach and said, "I want to move to the water. I want to live by the shore. It's time for us to move." She remembered feeling an ironclad peace with her words. No fear of a good thing ending crossed her mind. No sadness about leaving some of their close friends behind crossed her heart. It was time and she knew she needed to just pack up and leave.

Later that day, they pulled out a map of Florida, closed their eyes, swirled a finger over the southern part of the state and plopped a fingertip onto the sight of their future home. Neither of them had ever heard of Anna Maria Island, but thought the name was engaging and it was right on the big water; their only main requirement at the time.

In March of that year they spent spring break in Orlando visiting Mickey's world for a few days. After Disney, they headed over to Brandon to visit Jim's aunt and uncle, Fred and Sandi. At the time, Fred was a pastor in a local church. When they shared their plans of moving to Anna Maria, which was only forty minutes away, Fred asked about work. Jim was a private investigator at the time, working domestic cases, though he really wanted to be involved in insurance fraud. Fred told him a member of his congregation was a private investigator and had just told him he had been looking for someone to hire. A few phone calls later, the man came to Fred and Sandi's house, talked with Jim and hired him on the spot. Even more surprising, he specialized in insurance fraud. Bonus! Angela thought it was a perfect coincidence and that they were very lucky to have hooked up with the right people. Everything seemed to be following the perfect plan for them to move to south Florida.

In May, they returned to Anna Maria to explore the town, learn their way around and find a place to live. Angela was also planning to attend a job fair for the Manatee District School System hoping to find a new school for teaching kindergarten. She had done a little research online about which schools looked awesome and those she should avoid like the plague. She entered the civic center aimed with high hopes and a battle plan but as it turned out, she couldn't choose which principal she would get to talk with. Bummer. Instead, all the applicants were lined up and entered a room single file. The principals were at individual tables, and the applicants were randomly paired for an interview.

Potluck

Angela was at the end of the line and paired with a principal from a school that she knew was on the "plague" list, which wasn't very encouraging. She remembered thinking, *You've got to be kidding. I drove nine hours with a three-year old to end up with this type of potluck interview. This is not what I had in mind.* She put on her best teacher face, opened her portfolio and poured her heart out. The principal seemed to be mildly interested but as soon as Angela was done, she thanked her and indicated the interview was over. It did not look promising, and Angela was crushed.

She was waiting in the lobby of the civic center for Jim to pick her up when she noticed a few people rushing through the crowd like blood hounds searching for someone. Angela realized it was the principal she had talked with, and she had a man in tow. Angela thought, *This ought to be good.*

They rushed over to her and, out of breath, the man explained that he was opening a new school and was looking for a few more teachers. He wasn't able to interview Angela as he had to get back to the next round of applicants, but he wanted to know if she would sign a contract. In a flash, right on the spot, he couldn't promise her a kindergarten class but he could place her somewhere. She accepted before anyone could change their minds and again, believed that good juju was on her side. In June, they packed up and blasted off to a new life.

During the months prior to their move, Angela never had a doubt that this was the right thing to do. Both Angela's and Jim's parents, who lived about an hour and a half away from their college hometown, were heartbroken. Ashley was the prized first grandchild on both sides, and they weren't very excited about her being so far away. Still, Angela had bulletproof peace about the move even though she couldn't explain it logically. Everything that seemed important in their first attempt to move now felt trivial. This time was different. This time was right.

A Whispered Warning

The next few years sailed along and life was heavenly. They had another daughter. They found a local community church that was new and growing rapidly. It was in this place, a school by weekday, a church by weekend, that Angela began to grasp the importance of what a relationship with God could bring to her life.

In the winter of that year, their daughter Ashley was twelve and in middle school. Though there was no odd behavior going on, Angela had this uneasy sense that something wasn't quite right with her daughter. She couldn't put her finger on it but she felt that familiar whisper from God again. Feeling that it was maternal instinct, she told Jim what was going on so they watched closely. They checked her texts and watched her Facebook page, but nothing was amiss. Angela shared her concerns with a dear, Christ-following friend. Her friend said, "When I sense something is not right, that's God whispering to my heart telling me to pay attention."

Angela had never thought of that before. Her feelings of peace, or lack thereof were communication with God? This was new. She began to ponder the idea that maybe something wasn't right inside her daughter, not on the outside.

In February, Ashley tried out for the middle school worship team at their church and made it. Angela and Jim were so excited for her, and she was blown away to be included in the band. Over the next few months, she attended rehearsal faithfully every Thursday night and performed many weekends in a row. To Angela, it was strange for anyone to perform so often but for whatever reason, the leader kept requesting her to be there. Ashley developed a relationship with the main worship leader, taking in every word he had to share.

Not What You May Be Thinking

One night as Angela tucked her into bed, she noticed notes in Ashley's Bible. Asking Ashley about them, she told her mom that the worship pastor had said, when reading her Bible, to write her thoughts about what she read. She explained that he said it would help her to understand God's word. *Wow*, Angela thought, *I'm her mother and I never told her that. I don't even do that myself.* Angela read her Bible, but take notes? She felt a twinge of guilt but a wealth of pride in her daughter and Ashley's passion to know God.

Angela began to notice over the next few months that her feelings of concern for her daughter began to subside, though she didn't have an explanation. Thinking of her friend's words about the whisper, she decided God didn't have anything else to say. Either that or it hadn't really been a whisper after all.

After All

In July, the mother of one of Ashley's friends called with very heavy news. She had found letters their children had written in January and February that outlined plans to engage in unsavory activities that had the potential to ruin both of their lives. Both moms were brokenhearted and shocked. Neither of them could believe the content of the letters or the idea that their children, both raised in church-going families, would even entertain these awful thoughts.

Suddenly, it hit Angela like a brick. These letters were written during the time when she had sensed that lack of peace and knew something was wrong! Her friend was right. God was whispering in Angela's ear. God knew Ashley was considering Satan's evil pressure in her life and God wanted Angela to protect her but she didn't realize what she was hearing. What a gut check Angela had.

Angela said, "I totally missed the whisper, but, thanks to God, the worship leader didn't." Once Ashley became involved with the worship team, the letters stopped. In fact, Ashley and this friend had stopped hanging out together around early May. As Angela was taking this all in, she realized God had shrewdly reached down and protected Ashley with people that weren't blood family but were faith family.

"Concentrate...on hearing the Lord speak to you...ask Holy Spirit to help you hear the truth."

~Dr. Gregory Boyd, *Seeing Is Believing*

Now Angela is reading and writing as she meditates on God's word, the Bible. She grabbed the idea that life isn't about luck or who you know or maternal instinct. Life is about going after God and asking Him, through Dangerous Prayers, to guide you and supply you with the answers you need. Angela asked me once how you know something is right, how you know when God is saying yes to a decision that feels right.

I told her, "It's not just a feeling. It's a peace in your gut. That peace is the Holy Spirit leading you. If something is not from God, you won't have that complete peace about the situation."

When Angela and Jim first wanted to move to the coast, there wasn't peace. Though she wasn't talking to God then, or asking for His guidance, He was there, letting her know it wasn't His plan for them. Now she understands that they were forcing the plan, not looking to God for direction. When they wanted to move to south Florida a few years later, Angela still wasn't talking to God or asking for His guidance, but He was helping them. He gave Jim and Angela an ironclad peace in their move because it was part of His plan. The new life they made there has very clearly been by His design. When their daughter was in trouble, Angela was seeking God more by reading His word but not as deeply as she could. He was still there, whispering in Angela's ear and guiding her heart.

Angela said, "I've come to believe that throughout my faith journey God has always been there. It's never been about who I know, or good juju, or the stars aligning. It's always been about God's plan for my life, whether I was acknowledging it or not. I don't hear God's voice audibly, so I have to be still and listen with my heart."

Angela Listens for God's Dangerous Whispers.

Psalm 46:10 NKJV says, *"Be still and know that I am God..."* When Angela was able to stop her everyday thoughts and focus on God, she could separate her natural desires from the Lord's desires. Her internal peace is the result and amazing assurance that her life choices were on the right path. Through Dangerous Prayers, Angela is able to move forward and live out God's plan for her life with real peace.

Our Guardian

My friends Angela and Jim learned to be guided by their peace, not who they knew or even coincidences like getting the job.

Sometimes when you get what you want, you can mistake it for God's answers to your Dangerous Prayers. God always answers your Dangerous Prayers with peace first, then the thing you ask for happens. It's not the other way around.

You don't live in a world completely ruled by God. You have an enemy here. He specializes in half-truths. He is called "the deceiver" of Christ followers, but he is no match for when God whispers. Philippians 4:7 NIV states:

"And the peace of God, which transcends all understanding, will guard your hearts and your minds in Christ Jesus."

This peace of God stands guard over you like a commando, protecting you from being deceived. When you are guided by your peace, not only your thoughts and emotions, God will always answer your Dangerous Prayers. God whispers come with a strong sense of either peace or unsettledness. It's not emotional or even logical sometimes, but like God did with Angela and Jim, He can guide you through life's adventures, too, if you will just listen for those whispers.

Charmed Life

In the next chapter, you will be exposed to the truth that you live in a world filled with uncertainty and that things can go from great to horrible almost overnight. For Ryan, "It was one of the few times in my charmed life that I felt hopeless and pessimistic about the future."

PRAYER ELEVEN
The More You Know

Your only limitation is your working knowledge of God's ways. The more you know the more powerful your prayers become.

Without Any Warning

You don't always have to go looking for trouble. Sometimes it finds you, but it always comes with an amazing opportunity to learn from God. Sometimes trouble just appears without any warning. You may think living on the sidelines of life is safe and risk-free, and it may be for a while, but eventually you find yourself in scary situations that are bigger and more god-awful than you can handle on our own. It's in these times that you can hide your head in the sand or blame God and turn your back on Him, or you can engage Him and start the honest process of learning from Him.

Ryan

"Every adversity, every failure, every heartache carries with it the seed of an equal or greater benefit." ~ Napoleon Hill

My friend Ryan found himself in a nerve-shattering situation almost overnight. The situation seemed totally out of his control, strangling the life out of everything from his finances, his family and even more, his faith in God.

To use his words, "It was one of the few times in my charmed life that I felt hopeless and pessimistic about the future."

Life Really Sucks Right Now

It was in the fall of 2009. Ryan's company, a technology firm, had been in business for over ten years. It had survived the burst of the dot-com bubble and some of the most difficult, helpless economic conditions this country had ever seen. Ryan and his team had spent the last six years building an awesome client relations software system and had some moderate success selling it in the Human Resource outsourcing market. The software they owned was a picture perfect fit for the needs of the industry and had tiny competition. However, the economy was tanking, and the HR outsourcing industry keeps pace with the success of small businesses, which were failing at a dangerous rate. Ryan said, "Our backs were really up against the wall."

The company's bank account was nearly bone dry, and their credit line was jacked up, having just been called by the creditor. The elite team that once numbered twenty-six professionals was down to three, and still the company could not make ends meet. Ryan's personal wealth had been squeezed hard over the years, trying to raise a family of six on a shriveling income. His family had saved enough money to weather the storm for a while longer, and for that he was grateful. Many friends were out of work with no decent job prospects and no savings to cushion the blow. Ryan made the decision to give up his salary for the fourth quarter of 2009 to give the company a fighting chance at survival.

As can be imagined, the crushing difficulties at work bled over to a mountain of stress and tension at home for Ryan and his family. His marriage was numbingly tense, and raising teenagers along with little ones was expensive and stressful. Life balance and rest was not a priority, nor was focusing on his relationship with God. Other activities that might give him peace and energy were non-existent. Kelly, his wife, had lost both her grandmothers earlier that year, and Ryan's own mother's health was in a rapid decline. His dad, at eighty, struggled to care for her. Needless to say, the stress in Ryan's household was so thick you could cut if with a knife.

Lightbulbs

"When I am through learning, I am through."

~Coach John Wooden

Earlier that year, Ryan had joined a men's Bible study that I was leading. We called the group "Lightbulbs" and we dove in deep to discover God's amazing grace and how we could use its ancient secrets in our daily lives. Ryan said to me, "Needless to say, this was good timing, not just for me, but for many of the men in the group."

The Lightbulbs group was immersed in studying scripture, encouraging and praying for one another and trying to live out many of the ancient tactics we learned. Ryan learned some powerful lessons from this group, and all of them were tied back to these untapped scriptural promises and up close and personal revelations:

1. Realizing the importance of knowing that God can be in control when we let Him and that we need to rely on His strength and ability instead of our own.

"No branch can bear fruit on its own. It must remain in the vine. Neither can you bear fruit unless you remain in Me." John 15:4

2. Knowing that with God's grace (unmerited favor), through the sacrifice of Jesus Christ and empowered by the Holy Spirit, we can live a mortal but supernatural life while on this earth.

"I tell you the truth, anyone who has faith in Me will do what I have been doing. He will do even greater things than these because I am going to the Father." John 14:12

3. Understanding the importance of making our God-sized dreams so real to the point that we can feel, see, taste and smell them.

"Therefore I tell you, whatever you ask for in prayer, believe that you have received it and it will be yours." Mark 11:24

4. Truly believing that the Lord is crazy in love with us and wants to be very generous to us without fanfare or drama will carry us through hardships.

"The Lord is my rock, my fortress, and my savior. He is my shield, the power that saves me and my place of safety." Psalm 18:2

5. Utilizing the secret power and healing that are hidden within Holy Communion and anointing with oil.

"So Jesus said to them, 'Truly, truly, I say to you, unless you eat the flesh of the Son of Man and drink His blood, you have no life in you." John 6:53

"And they cast out many demons and anointed with oil many who were sick and healed them." Mark 6:13

Things Got Difficult

During this group, I warned the members that as we dive deeper into discovering God's tangible plan for our lives and we start focusing more on serving God, we should expect to attract the attention of a very real enemy. Satan realizes that the more entwined we are with God's Word, the less able he is to separate us from God's tangible plan for our lives.

The enemy was relentlessly attacking what seemed to be every area of Ryan's life. If it hadn't been for his stout faith in Jesus Christ and the gargantuan grace (strength) provided by his Father in Heaven, he would not have been able to withstand this siege of rapid attacks.

"The thief comes to steal, kill and destroy but I came that they may have life and that more abundantly." John 10:10

Though the enemy was relentless, Ryan had a new armory of weapons of his own, which he decided to release into battle. He remembers walking through his house one day anointing every room and chair with anointing oil. He did the same with his office. He spent time every morning with his Lord and took communion often. He wrote scripture on index cards sorted by topic, which he used to memorize God's Word so it would be readily available when he needed it. His words were laced with the promised wisdom of his God.

When he had an important phone call or meeting, he would bow and pray beforehand asking the Holy Spirit to take control and give him extreme favor among those attending. Though his family was living off savings and his wife's part time, preschool teacher's salary, he continued to promptly bring his tithe every Sunday, returning to God what was His.

Ryan had two very large prospects that were mounting interest in his software in the fall of 2009. Though he had asked and believed that His God would help him win both opportunities, at least one of them had to seal the deal in order for the company to stay afloat. Knowing there was nothing left in his power that could change the situation, he said, "I had lost all hope in my own abilities, leaving me to rely on God." Ryan had nowhere to go and learn but to the big boss himself, his Father in Heaven.

Throwing In The Towel

"But those who wait on the Lord will find new strength. They will soar high on wings like eagles. When they run they

will not grow weary. When they walk they will not grow faint." Isaiah 40:31

Ryan made a trip to Houston to the make a deal with one of these prospects. His contact, Sam, had not been very encouraging because they were close to signing a contract with another vendor. Still, he agreed to amass his team of decision makers to take a look at Ryan's software. As Ryan took the elevator up to their office, he asked the Holy Spirit to take control. He asked that his words be His words and for the Holy Spirit to wear him like a glove. He asked the Holy Spirit to give him relaxation and poise and to influence the hearts and minds of the people in the meeting to welcome his message.

The presentation went extremely well. As Sam walked Ryan out to his car he told him, though he couldn't promise anything, he was fascinated with Ryan's software and could tell the other decision makers were as well. Ryan flew back to Tampa thanking God for His strength, confident that God was arranging all things for Ryan's finest hour to date.

About two weeks later, after multiple failed attempts, Ryan finally reached Sam. Sam thanked Ryan for making the trip to Houston and gave him confidence that his software was solid, but as they were too far along with the other contract, they would not be inking a deal with Ryan's firm.

Ryan had really been looking forward to bragging about how God came through to his buddies in the Lightbulbs group. Instead, he felt like a failure as he delivered the bad news that things had become even more desperate. The anxiety of almost two months without a paycheck was crushing. Ryan was not producing for his family, and their lifeline was about to be cut. Was it time to throw in the towel?

"Is there any such thing as a miracle? Get your faith strengthened and you will see miracles happening. Indeed you will experience miracles."

~Norman Vincent Peale

Resurrection

Another colossal prospect out of Hawaii that had their toe in the water for a while was finally approaching a decision. It was a momentous opportunity. They would be paying license fees up front. The cash was sorely needed. Though Ryan was beaten down in his heart, he was full of faith that this deal would close and God would rescue his company from the bottomless pit. He would still have his opportunity to brag on his God to the group.

Countless phone calls and web demonstrations resulted in a personal request from his contact, Jim, for executable contracts. This was a big flag that a deal was inevitable.

Ryan said, "I remember my excitement and anticipation as I anointed hard copies of the contracts with oil before I sent the digital copies via email to Jim." The Lightbulbs group routinely prayed at the end of each meeting for the requests of the brothers in the group and this generous deal was clearly one that could use some of God's special assistance. We prayed as a group for God's favor and an immediate decision.

Christmas was bearing down and typically non-essential business would soon come to a screeching halt. About three weeks went by with mountains of unanswered phone calls and emails to Jim in Hawaii. Ryan finally got a word in early December. Though Ryan's product was big on their list as a future option, the project would be put on hold until the middle of next year at the earliest. Focus had shifted.

You've got to be kidding! Not again!

Ryan stepped into his office, shutting the door, terrified of what the future held, but prayed dangerously. He said to his Father in Heaven he didn't understand the test but then decided to lay his company and his future at God's feet, asking Him to lead and teach him to go wherever He wanted to take him. Then God answered Ryan's Dangerous Prayer. His answer was not what Ryan expected but he heard it loud and clear. Resurrection! Though the Hawaiian deal was flat-lined, with no pulse and no life signs, God told Ryan He would resurrect it. Ryan believed it would be resurrected, but not until the middle of next year, as Jim had said.

That Wednesday Ryan shared with our group what had happened but he confidently told us that the deal would be resurrected becoming a catalyst for dynamic growth for his company, his family and most importantly his FAITH.

The following Tuesday he received an email from Jim, letting him know that his firm might be the best possible fit for a dire need they had for reporting, which had never crossed Ryan's mind. If he agreed, they would take the deal immediately. At that point, Ryan said he would have agreed that his firm could launch the space shuttle! God not only delivered on His personal promise to Ryan, *Resurrection,* but he did it in an instant, which Ryan had thought was impossible. The verse in Mark bears repeating:

"Therefore I tell you, whatever you ask for in prayer, believe that you have received it and it will be yours." Mark 11:24

The lucrative opportunity had been dead, and with it nothing to cling to for Ryan's company. Now, he had a lifeline straight from Heaven. He couldn't wait until the next Lightbulbs meeting. He called me and several other brothers to tell us the God-sized news. He told me, "I was as excited about the testimony I could give as I was for the financial impact of the deal."

"If God is with us, who could stand against us?"
Romans 8:31

With that lifeline came a massive boost of momentum. Ryan's company thrived through a situation so dire that the only explanation of how they made it is by God's jaw-dropping power. They started the year 2010 with a huge amount of wind in their sails and proceeded to have a solid, lucrative year paying back Ryan's missed paychecks, negotiating new terms on a loan with their bank and even making a profit for the year. Momentum mounted into 2011 as they had their best year since the glory days of the dot-com boom of 2001. Ryan's personal income rose by 30%, the firm made a six-figure profit, and the mind numbing stress at home had finally evaporated.

He Will Never Leave You

As 2012 launched, Ryan spent focused time reflecting on 2011. He applauded God asking Him to brilliantly light up the path He wanted him to take. The scripture He gave Ryan was Psalm 127:1.

"Unless the Lord builds the house, they labor in vain who build it. Unless the Lord guards the city, the watchman stays awake in vain."

Ryan said, "I believe this was God's way of reminding me where this incredible testimony came from Him. That it had nothing to do with my abilities, our software or even luck. It was God's love for me and His grace that landed me where I was."

Ryan decided to serve God and pray Dangerous Prayers more intentionally in late 2012, and he started his own men's ministry. He called the group "Brothers" and that group still meets regularly today. Under Ryan's leadership, the group stands arm-in-arm serving God, pushing the limits of each other's faith, mining His Word for secret answers and putting the devil on notice that he has already been defeated by our risen Savior.

Ryan's business continues to rock and break old company records. Setbacks do happen, both personally and professionally, but he is reminded of the pit from which God rescued him and knows God is standing right beside him and will never leave him. "Now where did that mountain go? I'm ready to see God move it," is Ryan's statement of faith. Ryan knows how to pray Dangerous Prayers that cause him to learn God's powerful ways.

God's Ways Are Gargantuan Compared to Our Ways

There is no trust without risk. Sometimes you can decide to trust when you find yourself in situations that are out of your control. Sometimes you can even create these situations for yourself. Either way, like my friend Ryan, you can learn from God if you want to develop life-giving, mountain-moving, Dangerous Prayers. You must learn:

"For my thoughts are not your thoughts, neither are your ways my ways, saith the LORD. As the heavens are higher than the Earth, so are my ways higher than your ways." Isaiah 55: 8-9 KJV

"Some things are hidden. They belong to the LORD our God. But the things that have been revealed in these teachings belong to us and to our children forever. We must obey every word of these teachings." Deuteronomy 29:29 GWT

Lori

With Lori, year after year, there was always a new issue to deal with. Lori lost her hair and began wearing a wig. It was as if her body was out of control and there was no stopping it. Not only had she been robbed of her quality of life, but it was also eating away at her husband and two children. Finally after thirteen years of suffering, she discovered a simple little Dangerous Prayer that restored her health and eventually changed her life. Lori's story is next, and it's one of my favorites.

PRAYER TWELVE
The Prayer Killer

Learn the dangerous principle that stops this insidious killer of prayers.

Lori

This is the story of Lori's simple Dangerous Prayer that produced sweet victory over her pain. She suffered for thirteen long miserable years before her prayers were answered and she was healed. Her acute pain was both physical and emotional. And not only did her sickness almost devour her alive, but it slowly chewed up happiness and joy from her husband and children's lives as well.

Even though Lori now enjoys a vibrant life and restored body, her story holds a life-giving lesson that is as much about a critical Dangerous Prayer principle as healing. Sometimes the answers you are seeking for your prayers don't come, and that can be a serious symptom of something much deeper and more deadly that God wants to reveal and stop dead in its track so that you can be truly healthy and whole.

"My beloved friend, I pray that everything is going well for you and that your body is as healthy as your soul is prosperous." 3 John 2 The Voice

Flu-Like Symptoms

Back in April of 1999, Lori was diagnosed with an autoimmune disease called dermatomyositis. It all started with flu-like symptoms but quickly, in just one year, Lori went from being a very active person to not being able to feed or bathe herself. Regrettably, it didn't stop there. The following thirteen years became a sickening roller coaster ride.

Dermatomyositis was such a rare disease that it took a number of months for her rheumatologist to diagnose her. Lori's rheumatologist was an angel and had been there with Lori from the very beginning. She saw Lori through the worst time of her life. She never gave up and was always driven to go the extra mile to make sure she had not left one stone unturned. If she didn't have an answer, with God's help, she would search until she had one.

These common, flu-like symptoms had developed into a swollen face and feet. Lori's feet were so swollen that the skin burst open and bled, making it very demanding just to walk at times. Her face had begun to swell until her eyes looked shut. In addition, she had heliotropes—reddish purple discoloration on her eyelids—another one of the unusual symptoms of this wicked disease.

Lori's mouth was so raw with sores that she had to use "magic mouthwash." She would swish the medicated mouthwash around in her mouth right before eating so that the pain was tolerable when she made an attempt to just eat soup. By this time, her esophagus had partially closed up, making it hard to swallow anything, even a cup of water. The disease advanced into severe pain between her shoulder blades as she struggled to swallow. Life had become unbearable.

Unusual Medicine

Year after year, there was always a new nasty issue to deal with. She lost her hair and began wearing a wig, and for someone so young—in her thirties—life was so depressing that all she wanted to do was stay at home and hide. Hidden away in her house, sometimes she would just stare out the windowpanes, watching life pass her by. "It was as if my body was out of control and there was no stopping it," Lori said. At one point, she had lost so much blood that the option of a blood transfusion was being discussed. Test after test had been done, and no one could determine the cause of the severe bleeding. Finally, after a colonoscopy, endoscopy, and partial hysterectomy were done, the excessive bleeding stopped.

One of the treatments she received for dermatomyositis was the controversial and very expensive IVIG injection. The use of this procedure at this particular hospital was so rare that the only place they had to put her while undergoing treatments was on the infant's floor so that she would have the attention of a nurse with only one other patient. This treatment was delivered in two four-hour intervals. In the pharmacy, assistants had to take turns standing and stirring the medicine for a continuous eight hours non-stop. Only once, a pharmacist stopped stirring and they had to throw the entire batch out. At the time, the compound was so rare and expensive that the hospital pharmacy didn't keep extra in stock, so she had to stay another day just to receive the treatment.

No Time To Waste

After her release from the hospital, Lori had constant doctor visits. In order to know which way the disease was progressing and to be on the lookout for side effects, lots of blood had to be drawn. It was not uncommon for eight tubes to be drawn in one office visit and sometimes she had to do this two to three times a week. This was not including the visits to other doctors. Once, Lori was admitted to the hospital for some tests and her veins collapsed. After the test came back she was immediately rushed to emergency surgery. On the way, she had been given pain medications to take effect before surgery but the doctor decided there wasn't time to waste.

He immediately tilted the bed so her head was pointed towards the floor. All of a sudden, Lori felt a sharp object slice across her skin. The nurses were screaming at the doctor to wait. He told them to shut up, and he proceeded to open the left side of her chest to install a Medi-port. By the time he finished with her she began to drift off, the meds taking affect. The next thing she remembers was waking up in her room.

Cancer?

She was diagnosed with IGA Nephropathy, which is an autoimmune disease that affects the kidneys, so she was sent to a nephrologist. She had also started bleeding again. Without any lab work or other tests, the doctor told her she had cancer. This diagnosis was totally out of the blue and had nothing to do with the problems she was having. She told the doctor this, and he finally sent her for lab work. When she returned for her follow-up visit, he informed her that there was nothing wrong with her. Now totally confused, she spoke to her rheumatologist, who referred her to a different nephrologist. Little did Lori know, the two doctors worked for the same group, just in another office and under a different business name.

The new nephrologist decided to talk with the first nephrologist she had seen. The new nephrologist concluded again, without any labs or tests, that there was nothing wrong with Lori. After much debate, Lori persuaded the doctor to do a simple urine test. The lab technician thought Lori was having her monthly period because of the large amount of blood in the urine sample. The tech was in shock when Lori informed her that there was no possible way for her to have a monthly period. No one seemed to think this was a sign of a problem, and still, both nephrologists were determined there was nothing wrong.

Lori's rheumatologist was not in agreement and finally persuaded the nephrologists to do a kidney biopsy. By this time, Lori's urine had turned the color of tea. The biopsy had shown that the filters in her kidneys were damaged which was allowing the kidneys to leak protein and blood. Even so, the nephrologists did not feel the need for treatment, concluding it was just one of the symptoms of the disease.

Yet Another Opinion

Through a family member, Lori met the most wonderful nephrologist at Baptist Hospital in Winston-Salem, North Carolina. The first time she met her, she reminded Lori of her angel—her rheumatologist. At the time of the first visit, Lori's scalp on the back of her head was raw and bleeding, clearly infected. Each year seemed to bring yet another bleak medical issue to deal with. She had to cut her hair extremely short so that it would just be easier to keep clean. After the appointment with the nephrologist, she saw a dermatologist there at the hospital. His diagnosis was psoriasis. He gave her a small bottle of medicine and in a couple of days, the oozing had stopped.

Trying To Survive

There were times throughout those miserable thirteen years that Lori just wanted to throw in the towel and just give up. Her prayers seemed to be hitting the ceilings and going nowhere. She told me, "Not only had my life been stolen from me, but it was horribly affecting my family." Now she wasn't the wife and mother she had always wanted to be. As each day came and went, she was just trying to survive. At her children's school events, she watched other parents and how differently they were treated, always being asked their opinions or to participate in activities. She was very overweight and most often had to wear a wig. She barely had enough strength just to make it to the function, much less help out.

People would sometimes ask her about her health. When she would tell them she had dermatomyositis, most of the time they would respond with something like, "Oh, I thought it was cancer." What was really sad was that most of these people were active in their church, but not one person ever asked Lori if she attended a church and never invited her to theirs. She was suffering in a pit of silence and desperation with no one reaching out to her other than her immediate family and her doctors.

At the end of her rope, she decided the guilt and misery of not being able to take care of her family and have her life back was too heavy to bear any longer. They deserved so much more. She decided she would end her miserable existence by overdosing with pain medication that had been prescribed to her. Despondent, she nervously opened the bottle and proceeded to swallow a handful of pills. Her husband walked in and tried to grab the bottle, finally taking them from her. During the struggle, he realized her mouth was full of pills and he began to pry her mouth open with his fingers. He was a first responder with the local fire department, but it in no way prepared him for this gut-wrenching moment.

Lori's young daughter came into the kitchen just in time to see what was happening. Horror gripped her, and she began to panic and scream in fear for her mother. That's when Lori stopped dead in her tracks and quit struggling with her husband. "I will never forget that moment when I saw the horror in my daughter's face," Lori said.

A Reason to Stay in the Fight

There were family members who helped as much as they could. Her mom was great. She tried to help maintain some sort of normalcy in Lori's home by helping with cooking and cleaning. It was hard for Lori's mother to watch her daughter struggle with the things that most people take for granted, like simply swallowing a sip of water. Others who knew them saw Lori's family falling apart, but didn't want any part of the drama. It was too messy and inconvenient to deal with.

Lori felt as if she had become such a public embarrassment to her family. Eliminating her existence seemed to be the logical answer until she saw the pain in her daughter's eyes. After that day, she knew she couldn't leave her. She found her reason to stay in the fight.

On her good days, she did her best to function as a normal wife and mother. She went on school trips, attended teacher's meetings, saw her children off to the prom and attended their graduations.

The Prayer Killer Uncovered

In 2011, Lori was watching television early one morning. When the program was over, she got up to start her daily chores but forgot to turn the television off. As she was working, she began to listen to a minister on the television. He was teaching on Mark 11:23-25. She had heard this passage many times and even had it memorized, however, when the minister finished reading it, something innocent and pure stopped her in mid thought. *Forgiveness* was all that she could hear inside.

"And when you stand praying, if you hold anything against anyone, forgive them, so that your Father in heaven may forgive you your sins." Mark 11:25 NIV

Lori got it! She had bitterness, anger and resentment in her heart. Some of it was even toward God. Even though she had become a Christ follower at the age of thirteen and truly loved God, Lori's life with Christ had become lopsided with un-forgiveness. She strained her mind to remember when, but at some point, she took her eyes off God and put her faith in people. Some of the people who hurt her the most were her church family. Using that as an excuse, she stopped going to church completely except for an occasional visit at holidays or special events. She had become bitter, and it was eating her physically from the inside out. Her prayers were dead.

Lori's Dangerous Prayer

"My life was crumbling," she said, "I didn't know where to turn anymore." That morning in 2011, Lori stopped what she was doing, sat down, and began to weep. She knew it was time to pray a Dangerous Prayer, a prayer to forgive. She began to name each and every person she needed to forgive. She didn't realize until that moment how much resentment she had been harboring. "This time it was the Holy Spirit helping me to forgive," she said. "I also, for the first time, understood that unforgiveness was making me sick, and forgiveness was going to help me heal."

"Lord you know what _____ did to me. It was wrong and very painful, however, Lord, I choose to forgive _____ for what they did and to release them. Lord, I ask you to forgive them for what they did. I ask you to forgive me for judging them and holding unforgiveness and hate in my heart. I refuse to live the rest of my life in bitterness. Lord, release me from the sin of judgment so that I may live free and full of joy. Thank you, Lord. In Jesus Name."

After that eye-opening morning, Lori's private time with the Lord went back to the top of her list again. She started spending hours each day studying the Bible and praying. She would rummage through the scriptures to find ancient promises for her life. She was desperate to personally know what God's promises were. She said, "I knew I had a choice to make. His word said, *'I set before you life and death; choose LIFE'*. Life is in His words."

She had read the Bible many times but this time was different. She began devouring the scriptures that pertained to God's secret truths about healing and health. She would confidently speak these scriptures out loud to God and over her life and body during her prayer time. She said she claimed them as authentic and relevant for her life and refused to let go of God's promises. In a short time, Lori knew in her heart that her body was getting stronger and it was just a matter of time before her body would jump to the next level of health and wellness. Through learning God's ancient promises from the Bible, she created pictures in her mind and heart of what her body would look like.

Pain Meds

Once, on the way back home from a visit with family, her loving husband reminded her that she would need to get her pain medication refilled the following morning. He was always good about helping her to remember those things because he had seen first-hand for over a decade the excruciating pain she had experienced. A few times over the years, Lori had run out of her meds over a weekend and had to live through the white-hot pain for a day or two. His kind and caring heart broke for his precious wife when she was in pain.

But this time was different. Lori turned to her husband and said, "I don't need the medication anymore." She was just as shocked as he was. Did she really just say that? What was she thinking? He began to plead with her to get the prescription filled just in case, but she knew without a shadow of a doubt in her heart, now was the time. So on January 1, 2012, she completely stopped using her pain medications and she never used them again.

But that's not the end of the story.

Not Over

Lori didn't realize that the next two months would be spent dealing with severe withdrawals from the pain medicines that had been in her system since 1999. There were days that the only thing she could remember were the hot baths she would take to help ease some of the withdrawal pain. Months before, she had picked about ten Christian songs and downloaded them to her iPhone. Little did she know at the time that these songs would become crucial to her recovery.

There were days that she couldn't open her mouth to pray or quote scripture but she could put these songs on shuffle and just let them play over and over. She would lie there silently praising God for His amazing promises of healing while listening to "Amazing Grace," "I Am Redeemed," and the other songs that were playing. Thoughts of doubt and unbelief would occasionally raise their ugly heads, but she would quickly slam the door on them and not allow them to take hold of her mind. She knew they were evil, not from her God!

Holy Spirit

After a few weeks into this process, an inner voice (Holy Spirit) told her to go online and see what vitamins and minerals would help in her recovery. Right away in her online search, she found a formula using vitamins and minerals that help with withdrawals from certain drugs. A man who had been in and out of drug rehabilitation had posted it in hopes it would help others. Sure enough, after about four days of taking this huge quantity of supplements, she was feeling like a new person.

In May, Lori had another crazy setback. She was diagnosed with gluten sensitivity. The test for celiac disease came back negative but as she had been off gluten for six weeks before the test, her rheumatologist told her that it was inconclusive. She could go back to eating gluten for a couple of months and repeat the test.

Lori's doctor explained that apparently there had been something in the pain medications she had been taking for so many years that had helped to mask the symptoms of gluten sensitivity. Now that she was off the meds, the allergy had magnified. Once she started eating gluten-free, the swelling in her face stopped, the blisters left her mouth, and she lost twenty-six pounds.

Letting Go

Lori's first step in receiving her healing was when she prayed dangerously to let go of the past and forgive. She had held on to the killer hurt for way too many years, and it had had been killing her prayers. God could hear and with love wanted to answer her prayers, but couldn't. So He pursued her many times and many different ways to help her see what her unforgiving heart was doing to her. It took a long time, and she finally caught the prayer killer.

Have there been opportunities for her to harbor bad feelings towards the same people since then? You bet! But now, Lori is much wiser and usually finds a way to be a blessing to those people. Why? She realizes how the unforgiveness was a deadly trap to empowering her illness, so she quickly forgives as much for herself as for others. But more importantly, there is nothing more valuable to her than the sweet relationship she now has with her Heavenly Father. She said, "Hasn't He forgiven each of us?"

"You asked for a loving God: you have one."

~C. S. Lewis, The Problem of Pain

Senseless Funerals

In all my years of being a pastor, I have many times found this one thing more powerful than prayer, and that's not forgiving others. It seems to be the greatest enemy to answered prayer. I have seen it rob people of their health, shatter their wealth, and rot their relationships and yes, even destroy their lives. I have officiated way too many senseless funerals from suicides than I would like to remember. Many of those people would not forgive others, and so they could not forgive themselves. Fortunately for Lori, she learned to forgive others, and in turn, forgive herself. And I might add, just in the nick of time, and I did not have to officiate her funeral.

So how about you? How's your health? How is your wealth? How are you and your relationships? Is there any deadly unforgiveness lurking around in your heart, hideously taking bites out of your health when you aren't looking? Maybe you are deciding not to forgive someone thinking, *I got this! Hey, they hurt me first so I'll just bide my time. I'll get them back when they least expect it.* What a trap! Yes, they hurt you, and you know what? You have a right to hurt them back. Yep! You read it right! But, forgiveness—real forgiveness—is when you decide to give up your right to hurt them back. Be dangerous and don't be normal. Pray

Dangerous Prayers of forgiveness. No more senseless funerals, please!

Trust: the Truth Ingredient of Dangerous Prayers

Have you ever tried to eat something without salt that was normally salty? Nasty! I'm from "grits country". We love grits in South Carolina. We love them with butter, eggs, bacon, fried pork chops, tomatoes, cheese, shrimp and even sardines, but not without salt. Nope, just not gonna happen. You definitely can tell when grits don't have salt. They taste bland and boring. Salt is the magical ingredient that makes most foods delectable.

Trust is much like salt for prayers. And just like when salt is absent in food, you can tell when trust is just not there in a prayer. Want to know how you can tell?

The prayer really never gets anywhere; it just kind of fizzles out over time. The prayer may start out like a white-hot fuse on the end of a piece of dynamite but when the fuse burns out, nothing happens! Everyone is left standing around with their fingers in their ears, all ready for something to happen, and there's nothing but a little smoke. How disappointing! Prayers will fizzle out and be very disappointing if TRUST is not a main ingredient. In Dangerous Prayer Thirteen, Rachel learned and experienced the exciting and explosive power of adding trust to her Dangerous Prayers. It gave Rachel one of her heart's desires, and he was just perfect!

PRAYER THIRTEEN
In God We Trust

Supercharge your Dangerous Prayers.

Lollipops and Rainbows

You cannot go through life without thinking at some point that the things that happen in your life with its twists and turns are just some random cosmic-roll of the dice. If good things come, then the moon and the stars must have aligned just right, and if bad things happen then obviously the gods are angry and out of control, again. There's no plan. You are only biding your time here on spaceship earth. All you've got is just some vague cosmic hope that things go well.

But there is something terribly wrong with this thinking. Instead of some cosmic roll of the dice, as a Christ follower, you have something far greater working on your behalf. You have a God who is entirely involved in your life right down to the numbering of the very hairs on your noggin. As a matter of fact, it even says so in the Bible in Luke 12:7 NIV:

"Indeed, the very hairs of your head are all numbered. Don't be afraid..."

The real question is, are you bear-hugging this truth or just cuddling it as some mumbo-jumbo? Is it *the gods must be angry* or does *The God*, I mean the real one in the Bible, have your back? It can mean all the difference between resting and stressing about the crazy stuff of your life. Someone a lot bigger than you knows all the challenges and opportunities you will face. How? He has a map—a map of your life. Would you like to know what's on the map?

Here you go.

"For I know the plans I have for you," says the Lord. "They are plans for good and not for disaster, to give you a future and a hope." Jeremiah 29:11 NLT

Now you have a real decision to make, say yes to the cosmic mess or yes to your God, who created you in love and wants to help you finish your life with hope. The truth is you don't really think about this kind of stuff until something hits the fan. But when it does, and it will, some of the stuff in this chapter may help.

You are probably way ahead of me right now or you might be asking, "Okay, so how do I do that?"

Glad you asked. With Dangerous Prayers, of course. It's the action of including in your Dangerous Prayers trust in the goodness of the heart of God. All throughout scripture, you can see story after story of how prayer and faith won monumental battles.

It's not just God doing His thing and you doing your thing. It's the two of you, through the Dangerous Prayers full of trust, working together. All healthy relationships are based on trust. God's relationship with you is no different. Only through trusting each other and working together in the darkest times can you achieve what seems to be impossible. Life is not lollipops and rainbows, so you're gonna need His help to overcome or get through your most difficult times. Trust Him. He is a good God and has a good heart. I know this from experience, and so does Rachel.

Rachel

Let me explain it a little better by telling you about Rachel's Dangerous Prayer life. Her many Dangerous Prayers of trust have changed her life when she was face to face with impossible situations. And in Rachel's case, what seemed like dead ends became the open doors to God's promises. She has come to know a God who is intimately involved with her life. She now confidently trusts that when her life is over, she will have arrived at all the checkpoints God had on her life's map and for the most part, in one piece.

Rachel knew which way was north on her life-map, to live as a Christ follower. What she did not know was where the hot deserts, alligator-infested swamps, dark, wet caves or refreshing oases and lush fruit-laden valleys were. But God did.

Her story begins back in May of 1983. That's when she met Rick, who introduced her to Christ. A man crazy for Jesus, his passion and excitement for God captivated her. She found herself starving to know God and falling deeply in love with Rick at the same time. What a combination. In a couple of very short months, they both knew that they would be married and that ministry was the life for them.

Michael Jackson Sings At Wedding...Kinda

They spent an insane number of hours talking about their life, their future and all the things that God had called them to do. They even talked about children. Rick, being from a family of six thought maybe they would have four boys. One would be enough for Rachel. She daydreamed about the one who would be the spitting image of his daddy.

By the following March, they were married. Nothing huge or glamorous, just the two of them with their parents and siblings at the Justice of the Peace's home with Michael Jackson singing *Thriller* on the radio in the background. No kidding! Michael Jackson sang at their wedding....kinda. The Justice of the Peace forgot to turn off the radio, and they didn't notice until the "I do's" were wrapped up. Great memory, and quite honestly a prophecy as their marriage has been a thriller, but I'm getting a head of myself. Now, where are we? Oh, yeah.

They quickly settled into married life. Though they talked about having children, they never really did discuss when. So without really thinking that part through, by September, BAM! Rachel was pregnant with their first child.

Since this was the first grandchild on both sides, the anticipation was crazy high. They couldn't wait to tell everyone. Rachel said she has never found a greater joy than to share the news of a baby coming into the world. She also found the opposing horror is also true when you have to tell everyone that you have miscarried.

Bring A Jar To The Hospital

She began miscarrying and so they quickly sent out requests for prayer. She hoped it was a false alarm. She was sitting on the couch one of those miserable evenings and praying, "God, please don't let this happen. God, you have to do something." As she sat there painfully crying out to God, she thought of the scripture in Genesis where the murderous Pharaoh had commanded that all the helpless Jewish baby boys be killed. Moses' mother, in order to protect her precious little child, had to carefully wrap him, place him in a basket, and float him into the crocodile-infested Nile River where he was later found by Pharaoh's daughter. What a miracle.

You probably know the rest of the story. Pharaoh's daughter's heart was moved with compassion for the tiny one, and so she decided to raise Moses as her own son. Years later, he became the liberator of the Israelites. As Rachel thought about Moses becoming an adult, God spoke to her heart. She said God told her He was able to keep safe any child that He had for her. In the face of how terrible it looked, He would protect her children.

Those few words from God did something powerful to Rachel's heart. She felt comfort. She really believed that this was a false alarm and that her baby would be just fine. However, when the doctor asks you to bring a jar to the hospital to put the remains of your child in, all your hopes and dreams evaporate. As the doctor was validating her deepest fear, she went numb and felt like every ounce of her energy was draining out on the floor in front of her.

Only those who have lived through a miscarriage can really connect to its sorrowful impact. Rachel was free falling from her great emotional high while her hormones were chewing her up from the inside out. She felt that God had flat-out lied to her. He had not kept His word and had not protected her child like she believed He would.

Giving Birth To Faith

Within a couple of months, the sadness began to wear away and she was pregnant again. She was somewhat excited and scared to death at the same time. She just couldn't bear another painful loss. *This time we won't tell anyone*, she thought, *so we won't have to wade through another round of explanations and gut-wrenching heartbreak if something were to happen again.*

Unlike the previous pregnancy, Rachel immediately got morning sickness, which according to her doctor, was supposed to be a good sign. "The healthier the pregnancy, the more likely you are to being sick," he said. Her comfort by the doctor words were short lived as she found that morning sickness turned into afternoon sickness and then afternoon sickness into night sickness. Quite honestly, she wanted to die. *It can't be worth it*, she thought.

Fortunately, the sickness didn't last long, and in September of 1984, little Faith made her grand entrance into their world. Rachel remembered her husband holding her in his arms in the delivery room and thinking how she looked much older than a newborn. Faith appeared to be looking around the room and demanding that someone turn the darn heat up. Yes, she had quite the imperial cry. The hospital nurses told Rachel that despite there being over twenty babies in the nursery that week, they could always tell Faith's cry because it was the most demanding. Faith's beautiful presence caused the pain of Rachel's prior miscarriage to become a very distant memory.

By the time Faith was about two months old, Rick and Rachel were quite ready to go out on a date. This new parents thing was getting in the way of some serious personal time together to say the least. Having only one income now, their budget was squeaky tight so they called the godparents, dropped Faith off, and went out for pizza. Upon leaving the pizza joint, they found a flyer on their car windshield that advertised a free movie showing at a local church. It was *The Cross & the Switchblade*, based on a radical young Pastor, David Wilkerson, going to NYC and starting what is now known worldwide as Teen Challenge. They didn't know much about the movie, but it was right in their budget, so they headed for the church.

Teen Challenge

That movie rocked their world. As they sat there, they could tell something was moving inside their hearts. Invisible hands changing things. Things that once were important to their future were now being replaced with new ideas and fresh passion. What was really crazy is that they dug around a few days after their date night and soon found a Teen Challenge about forty-five minutes from where they lived.

They called Teen Challenge and hightailed it over for a visit. While there, Rick and Rachel told them their story about their date night and the movie. They even offered to volunteer on weekends, and that's when it got really crazy. The big dog himself, the director, right on the spot offered Rick a job to be on staff. He would even give them a place to live there at the ministry.

Despite all the God stuff that was happening, they were not immediately convinced that Teen Challenge would be the place to cut their teeth in ministry. First of all, it would involve living on campus in the inner city—not the safest place for a young family. Then the "place to stay" was a house built in the 1800's with a somewhat rickety front porch and a questionable heating system. This was not the little white house with a white picket fence that Rachel had fantasized raising her newly born infant in, but after some prayer together she and Rick felt a peace about being a part of the Teen Challenge Team.

All seemed as it should be, that is until Rachel found out that she was pregnant again. What? So soon? Having been as sick as a dog with the previous pregnancy and having a demanding four-month old, Rachel wasn't entirely jumping up and down with joy and didn't think that Teen Challenge would be either after they got the news. However, when Rick called to inform them, they were excited and said, "The more the merrier." By Easter, they made the move.

Settling In

What an unsettling time for Rick and Rachel. Rachel now had to fine-tune her life to a new baby, a new house and a new round of morning sickness. Not to mention that a large part of the strength and support that had come from her best friend and husband, Rick, was now consumed as he was being baptized into a brand new phase of his life with ministry and its own set of daily challenges.

By November of that year, they were favored with another beautiful little girl, Noel. She was a beautiful complement to their family. Rick and Rachel were really crazy about their two little girls. It took about six years of working out the bugs of being in full time ministry, making a 180-year-old museum a home, and bringing up two energetic little bundles of love, before Rachel got the baby bug again.

It was a crazy idea. The girls had started school and Rachel was working part time at Teen Challenge, which helped heal their financial bottom line a little, but somehow she convinced Rick that they still needed to add to the family. Rachel still visited her recurring daydream of having a boy that looked just like his daddy. So within a very short time, Rachel became pregnant. Their little girls were absolutely giddy. Ecstatic, with ear-to-ear smiles and big bright eyes, they had to tell everyone at the following church picnic about the baby.

The Hardest Job in the Universe

While at the church picnic, Rachel started feeling horrible. She knew something wasn't right, so she told Rick and he gathered up the girls and they headed home. Rachel recalls lying in bed with an impending sense of *here we go again*. She had been flooded with a bounty of high hopes and excitement for this pregnancy. Everyone was celebrating the coming of the new baby, especially the girls. It was like waiting for Christmas day to arrive. How could Rachel and Rick bring themselves to explain to the girls that there would no longer be a baby to celebrate? How could they look into those beautiful little smiling, happy faces and say that? This had to be the hardest job in the universe.

Within the week, the doctor said that she had miscarried. To everyone's surprise, the girls took it really well. Rachel, on the other hand, was as crushed and heartbroken as she had been after her first miscarriage, maybe even more.

Her time of mourning was cut very short because within a few weeks after the miscarriage, she was pregnant again. At best, her doctor was cautiously optimistic, given her history, and decided to do an ultrasound on Christmas Eve just to confirm that everything was okay. Much to everyone's joy, Rachel and Rick saw the heartbeat on that Christmas Eve day. What a great Christmas present!

David Letterman Crush

This pregnancy seemed much different because of the baby's activity level. This baby was strong, too. Though they could never confirm the sex of the baby during any of the ultrasounds, Rick and Rachel were convinced that this baby was a little boy. They had names picked out and were eyeing little boy outfits every time they went shopping. It was midway through the pregnancy that it hit Rachel—*Is this one really a little boy or am I daydreaming again?* After some prayer and time with her source of strength through all those years, her Heavenly Father, she believed this baby was a girl and decided to name her Joy. If she was wrong and the baby was a boy, he would have a real problem growing up with the name Joy. As she smiled to herself, Rachel just knew it would be another little girl. And it was. Little Joy came on board the family on a hot August evening and rocked their world.

What a little doll! She was adorable and slept much of her first three days. And then she awoke and never slept another wink. Well, not much after that anyway...too much world to see. But Rachel loved it. It gave her more time to spend with Joy rocking her and enjoying her.

Rachel used to have a running joke that Joy had a crush on David Letterman because she would never go to sleep until after his show was over at 1 am. But then she would fall asleep in Rachel's arms. As Rachel would tenderly put Joy in her crib for the night she would think, *Now our family is complete*, or so it seemed.

Spiritual Wedgies

Rick and Rachel were utterly thrilled with the three little girls God had given them. As far as they were concerned, their quiver was full and their family complete. And though for years she had daydreamed of having a little boy just like his dad, she had decided it was best to release him and allow him to gently drift away as the time she had to daydream seemed to be absorbed by the day to day routines of life. She agreed to let herself become content with the blessings she had. But when the David Letterman fan, Joy, turned one and a half, something began to awaken in Rachel.

She suddenly became aware that even though her God-given daydream had been lying quiet for a very long while, it was now coming alive again and was beginning to stand up in her heart and demand attention. Rick had affectionately named those times spiritual wedgies. It's just when you know something is not quite right and God is compelling you to make an adjustment.

Rachel's spiritual wedgie started getting massive almost overnight when something got into the water system and there was a baby boom at Teen Challenge. All the staff wives were having babies within a few months of each other, and not just babies—baby boys. And not just baby boys, but juniors. There was John Jr., and Jeffy Jr. and Willie Jr. and then finally Benjamin Jr. Rachel was very happy for all the new moms, but something went supersonic in her when she went to the hospital to visit the fourth boy Junior. She thought, *where is my Junior?* Where is that little boy that God had painted on my heart?

Then common sense raised its head and she thought, *Where was this coming from? I was content. Having girls is great. Why am I feeling this way?*

Rachel left the hospital with a gut-wrenching sense of loss. She was sincerely happy for her friends but something was clawing at her insides, and the timing could not have been any worse. She was scheduled as the main speaker to a group of ladies at Teen Challenge that night. And strangely enough, her topic was "God Meets You at Dead Ends". *Why did this have to hit me today?* she thought. Her heart was heavy, and most of her life-giving nature seemed to be hiding somewhere in a corner of her heart, refusing to come out and help. She just didn't know how she was going to encourage these women.

She got to the offices prior to the meeting and spotted Karen, another Teen Challenge staff wife. She quickly grabbed her for prayer. Karen's husband, Eric, had served shoulder to shoulder with Rick for the last few years and they had become great friends. When they began to pray, Rachel began to cry. She just could not get through the prayer. She stopped sobbing long enough to say, "Karen, I have to share my heart with you."

Then Rachel spent the next few minutes pouring out her heart to Karen. Rachel felt such guilt for wanting a son because she truly was happy with the family God had given her. Karen simply smiled and said, "God can do that for you. Let's pray." Karen prayed one of the most beautiful, heartfelt prayers Rachel had ever heard, so full of trust in the goodness of God's heart. She simply asked God to give Rachel the desire of her heart. They left that room, went downstairs and God, by His grace, commissioned Rachel to share an engaging word of encouragement to the waiting ladies.

The Final Blow

After Joy joined the family, Rick and Rachel never really talked about having more children. But talking about it doesn't always matter, and much to Rachel's pleasant surprise, she found out that she was pregnant. Her heart told her that this was the little boy that had been in her dreams and tattooed on her heart since she and Rick had first discussed marriage. He would come and the family would truly be complete.

Not so. Within a few weeks, she suffered her third miscarriage. Each miscarriage delivered its own sickening sorrow and crushing disappointment to Rachel and Rick. Each one different but equally, wickedly painful but what Rachel was about to hear this time would break her already raw heart and challenge her and all that she thought she believed and trusted about God.

Her doctor, who knew her entire pregnancy and miscarriage history, summoned her to his office. The conversation went something like this. "Rachel, I believe you are miscarrying boys. I have seen this before. When someone has multiple children of one sex and then has multiple miscarriages, it's usually something wrong with either the male or female chromosomes. I could send you for chromosomal testing but it is very expensive. Quite honestly, if you do carry a boy full term, he most likely would be either severely handicapped or retarded. I know you really would like a boy but if I were you, I would consider adopting."

Rachel doesn't remember even saying goodbye as she slowly got up and left her doctor's office. She was so choked up. She said, "I felt like a ton of bricks had just crushed my heart." She could barely talk and was struggling just to breathe. Her mind kept playing the same question over and over again on her miserable ride home. *Why would I have this desire for a son that I trusted God had placed there if it wasn't going to happen?*

When she got home, her encounter with Rick was not a pleasant one for either of them. He innocently asked how her visit had gone, and the unexpected sorrow that had latched on to her heart at the doctor's office had turned to sour anger. She was angry with God. And she didn't mind letting both Rick and God know, either. She was just doggedly disappointed and frustrated. Fortunately, God knows our frame, and He did not leave her in that sad state of mind. God patiently allowed her to sort out her thoughts. He doesn't jump down your throat just because you get sideways with Him. He has a good heart.

Unlike the previous miscarriages, this one had a sense of finality to it. Rachel began to wonder if God was using the doctor to tell her something. Maybe this was all happening so that she would give in to an adoption. *Adoption is great*, she thought. She had not seen it during all the mind numbing experiences she had been through, but later realized how delicately beautiful God could put families together through adoption. *What a beautiful expression of God's love*, she thought. She even began to consider the possibility of raising three girls and willingly going forward with a chance to have a child that would be handicapped or retarded. She knew Rick and the girls would love the child regardless. It was never a matter of that. Her creeping concern was more the care and attention that would no longer be able to be focused on their three girls. She questioned the fairness of it all.

Praying Dangerously

Rachel spent the next few weeks in deep thought about what this all meant. She really struggled with it. In the depth of her heart, she trusted that God had a natural son for her but quite honestly did not know what delivery system He would use to deliver Junior. *How's God gonna pull this off?* That was the question.

As mentioned earlier, Rachel knew that Dangerous Prayers could change things. These are not nice little "headache" prayers that you pray over your Happy Meals hoping no one is watching. Dangerous Prayers reach out and grab your current circumstances, mix them with trust in God, and see amazing answers.

But you have to be unreasonably ready to pray Dangerous Prayers. In other words, you have to be so unreasonable that you won't take no for an answer. Sometimes even a little desperation can help get you there. Rachel was desperate. When people get desperate, they get real. They get honest. Mostly they get moving, and in her case, toward God, not away from God. Rachel went to church with a mission and purpose. That night at the altar, she prayed that type of prayer, a Dangerous Prayer full of trust. It changed everything.

It was a typical church service. There was a time of worship. The pastor gave a timely message, but Rachel's desperate mind kept itself well occupied. She was crystal clear why she was there that night and it was not for the message, as great as it was. When the altar was open for prayer at the end of service, she quietly went and knelt down to pray. She was fighting with her mind to find the right words. The right words were hiding somewhere in the dark corners of her mind and refused to come out and help, again. Since nothing was coming out, how was she supposed to get in agreement with God and get His help? It was then that she sensed a familiar, soothing comfort and rock solid strength kneel down next to her. It was Rick.

Rick and Rachel had been praying together since before they were married, but this time was it was different. "Instead of allowing me to pray alone, Rick felt led to come and pray with me. He asked me, 'What can I trust in God with you for?' I looked at him with a heavy heart and full of tears and said, 'I don't know how to pray. The doctor said that I can't or shouldn't have a boy, but I just have this strong sense that God can still do that for me. What should I do?'"

Now, it is important to note here that Rick never had the same heart's desire for a son. He loved having his three little girls and never felt he was missing out or deprived of something. This was entirely a desire of Rachel's heart and for the first time, he agreed to trust in prayer for Rachel's heart's desire. Their Dangerous Prayer went something like this:

"God, we know what the doctor has said. He is a wonderful doctor. We have every reason to believe that what he is saying is true. But, we know that you are bigger than the doctor and you can do all things. If you have a son for us, we know that you can bring it to pass so we trust you."

They thanked God in advance for answering their Dangerous Prayer and closed the prayer in the name of the Lord Jesus.

Michael

When they got up from that prayer, Rachel had a sense that she really did trust and leave it with God. The following peace inside her heart was for a good reason. God had heard their Dangerous Prayer, and because they chose to trust Him despite their circumstances, He honored their Dangerous Prayer. Within a few short weeks, Rachel was pregnant. Given her history, she was cautiously optimistic. She really needed to get fresh assurance from God.

It was on a Palm Sunday of 1995 when during the church service, she asked God a question. She said, "Lord, I need to know if this is the boy that I trust you have promised me." Over the years, Rachel had had many different encounters with God during her years as a Christ follower but this day what she heard was so clear that she had to write it down. She wrote it on her church bulletin and still has the bulletin to this day. She felt the Lord impress on her that it was a boy and that she was to name him Michael, which means, "Who is like God."

When man says no, God is still able. She also felt the Lord impress on her that he would be a peacemaker, which she did not entirely understand but wrote down anyway. What an amazing time with God.

Two weeks later, upon having an ultrasound, she was notified that she was having a boy. She could not wait to go home and show Rick and the girls the ultrasound and tell them the great news. Despite the joy she was feeling, it wasn't very long before she began to get thoughts of fear. With every passing month, when she would get an ultrasound, she would ask, "Does everything look okay?"

On a cold January morning, on Martin Luther King Jr.'s birthday, Michael was born. The first thing the doctor said to her was, "Rachel, you got your boy, and he is perfect."

She held him in her arms and cried tears of joy for over an hour. She had her son, but even more amazing to her was the trustworthiness of her God. God had heard her Dangerous Prayer and delivered what He had promised.

Michael is now seventeen years old and is still just perfect. But the most amazing thing to Rachel is how God has used this experience to shape so many other areas of her life. She has had dreams that seemed to miscarry but God has always resurrected them from the dead. The things that God has spoken to her and Rick in secret have come to pass. They still pray dangerously and trust for the things that God has ahead for them.

When Rachel thinks back to that sad night sitting on the couch miscarrying, and what God told her about Moses, she marvels at the thought that he protected each child that he had for her and that no weapon formed against them prospered. God is true to His promises and can be trusted.

Deal With the Fear

Not long ago I asked my wife a drilling question. "What would be the most important advice you could give to another person who just found out they had cancer?" She went completely silent for a few moments, then she looked straight into my eyes and without a hint of hesitation said, "Deal with the fear first." And in the next and final chapter I will share with you exactly how you can deal with fear, no matter what you are facing.

PRAYER FOURTEEN
Certainty

How to dismantled fear and replace it with faith.

Stunned

My wife, Kim, is now five years and three months cancer-free herself. When she and I found out she had cancer, it was a crushing blow. For a short time, we both went into a state of shock. At the time Kim was very active and healthy. It was August 2008 when our world turned upside down in only a few seconds. After a colonoscopy, we listened as Kim's GI doctor told us that she had colon cancer. It felt like someone had hit me in the chest with a thirty-pound sledgehammer. For a few seconds I couldn't catch my breath. As we continued to listen, Kim said that she felt a cold numbness begin to creep into her body and soul. We were stunned to say the least. We couldn't believe it, but what was even more puzzling is that her doctor was shocked as well. She was only forty-seven years old at the time and certainly not supposed to have cancer.

It just didn't make any sense. According to the doctor, colon cancer was either genetic or happened to people who were much older than she was. No one in her family had ever had any history of colon cancer to her knowledge. Needless to say, it was a surprise not only to us and to the doctor's, but to the entire family.

Panic, fear of the unknown and memories of her past are just a few of the emotions and thoughts that forced their way into Kim's mind when she was given the diagnosis. She immediately thought of our three children: Kayla, Evan and Victoria, and of me as well. She began to wrestle with the potential anxiety that we could all be living under as a family in the months to come due to the unsettling changes it would have in our daily lives.

In a practical sense, it was flat-out terrifying to her.

Kim immediately thought of her dad. Her father had been diagnosed with a different type of cancer and had died a few years earlier. The chemotherapy he received pulverized his immune system to the point that he was unable to fight off a simple virus. He woke up one morning with a temperature and thirty-six hours later, he was gone. It was so tragic for Kim. The suddenness and sadness of what happened to her dad tried to run rampant in her mind, creating more fear of what might happen to her.

Cancer is such a spine-chilling word. It produced in Kim, in her words, an "indescribable fear". Unless you have walked through cancer yourself, it is difficult to put into words the chain-reaction it can have in your life. When you look into your doctor's eyes and he is trying to speak something while hesitantly biting his tongue at the same time just to say, "You have cancer," it penetrates your being to such a deep level. Those three small words challenged Kim to take a long hard look at her life. "You have cancer" became something she had on her mind daily and at times, minute by minute.

She remembers wanting to deny that this was actually happening to her. She was harassed with thoughts of the unknown. She had no idea the impact of what she was about to live through and felt very small and lost. She didn't know all of the "what", but she did know "Who" ultimately would be guiding her on this particular path of her life's journey. Her success would totally hinge on knowing the goodness of God and knowing God loved her. She thought of Kari Jobe's song, *Steady My Heart*, and knew He was what her fragile heart needed more than anyone or anything else in the world. There are times in your life when no one can do for you what Jesus can.

Kim had to intentionally make a decision to trust God just like the writer of Psalms 18:2 NLT when he said; *"The Lord is my rock, my fortress, and my savior; my God is my rock, in whom I find protection. He is my shield, the power that saves me and my place of safety."*

Tattoo on Heart

On the way home from the doctor's office we were silent. We sat letting all of the questions run through our minds again. What does this all mean? What were her chances of survival? How would it affect her daily life? On and on the mind-numbing thoughts just rolled, until it became obvious to us that we were letting ourselves be led down the primrose path of fear.

So before all the emotions had time to settle in, Kim and I made some purposeful decisions. We both have been Christ followers since our teens and had studied the Bible for many years. We understood the power of the Words that God breathed through those who wrote it. Words like, "death and life are in the power of the tongue" as proclaimed in Proverbs 18:21.

So on our ride home, Kim made a Dangerous and bold decision in the face of her circumstances: she would refuse to allow the medical report to defeat her spirit or predict her future. Instead she would turn the tables on it. Instead of becoming a victim, she would become a victor. She chose not to entertain any thoughts of death in her mind, her heart, or her words. She would fight with all her might every thought or feeling of defeat and discouragement and declared instead to pray Dangerous Prayers of her faith in God's heart of love and power to rescue and heal her. As her husband and the spiritual covering for our home, I totally supported her decision.

Being in the ministry, we knew of too many stories of people who had died prematurely after being diagnosed with a life-threatening disease all because they gave up. They not only let their minds run rampant with thoughts of death but they spoke it out loud over their lives like a poisonous dust. They expected to die, and they did.

Kim and I believed their bodies began to shut down as a result of their own words turning invisible switches in their own bodies shutting down one bodily system at a time. They became victims of their own words and thoughts of death and despair just as much as the disease that was attacking their bodies. Their only hope was in their doctors and their treatments. Their words reflected the defeat that had already begun to take root in their hearts.

It reminds me of the story of a missionary who once watched a soldier get a tattoo by an elderly tattoo artist in Vietnam. The tattoo artist was finishing up as the missionary walked by and saw "Born to Die" flawlessly and permanently engraved on the young soldier's bulging triceps. After the soldier left, the missionary asked the elderly tattoo artist why someone would want such words permanently written on their body, to which the elderly man said in broken English, "Tattoo on heart before tattoo on body."

Somewhere on I-75

Kim's heart spoke victory and told her that she was not hopeless! She also knew to dangerously pray her way to victory. She served a God who is undefeated in the healing business and answering Dangerous Prayers. She committed to stick close to the Lord with courageous faith and to galvanize her mind to win the victory. To conquer cancer was a choice she knew she had to make from the beginning. She felt that her destiny hinged on that choice. William Jennings Bryan said, "Destiny is not a matter of chance, but a matter of choice. It is not a thing to be waited for; it is a thing to be achieved." She had a destiny that was still blossoming and a crystal clear purpose for living, so Kim made the choice to live!

Before we got home, somewhere on I-75, we prayed dangerously.

"Lord, we know we live in a fallen world and that sickness and disease is prevalent, however we refuse to give into the fear it can bring. We now stand against not only this disease but also the paralyzing emotions that are trying to take over our minds. Give us courage and clarity to follow the steps that we are trusting that you will set before us. Health is a divine blessing. Now use our good doctors as well as your miraculous hand to bring healing and restoration to my wife's body. In the name of Jesus our Lord and Savior."

With a cancer diagnosis, much consulting comes. Many decisions had to be made. Her doctor recommended that she consult with an oncologist and surgeon. After the appointment was made, then there would be a series of doctors' visits which included lab testing. Right on the spot, surgery was determined and scheduled within a three-week timeframe. Kim's world was spinning faster and faster.

God Got Busy

What we have learned during this almost five-year journey is: faith, hope and love give us an unfair advantage over fear. Fear doesn't stand a snowball's chance in the desert in the face of great certainty or faith. When you know inside your heart that you are going to win, then hope springs up. Not like a daisy in the cracks of your driveway but like an oak tree in the backyard where the kids' swing hangs. All this is possible when you have a loving relationship with God.

I mean, come on. Think of how you feel when you know that special someone is always calling and wanting to hang out with you. You know that love is strong with that one. It does bring confidence and puts a little spring in your step, a little "zippity" in your "doodah". Well, when trouble comes your way, who are you going to call? Those who love you the most, right? And the bigger your loved ones, the bigger the mountain you can move with them. Well, if you cultivate that kind of relationship with God, when you have a big mountain, then you have big help.

Fortunately for us we had been hanging out with God in a loving relationship full of a lot of trust for decades. It didn't happen overnight; the mountain-moving kind of trust and love grew year after year as we would go to our God with stuff.

The point here is that some people try to rely on their own knowledge, wealth, contacts and influence and most of the time it's enough to navigate the rapids of life. But on rare occasions more is needed, a lot more, to handle the death-dealing dirty little secrets life can throw at us. Sometimes we need God's help, and He loves to do His part.

God got quite busy with us. He lined up some of the finest physicians as well as a host of others to help us. But that's not all He did. The biggest miracle of all was His peace and guidance. I mean we could tell inside of our hearts when to say yes to that and no to something else even though logically and scientifically it made all the sense in the world. You see, what all our doctors and our friends and loved ones could not do was to hear from God for us, nor own the mountain of potential life and death decisions we had to make.

Our Mastermind Group

Napoleon Hill describes in his writings the importance of surrounding yourself with a close group of friends who will mutually help each other in the obtaining of personal goals. This mastermind principle is equally powerful when one is confronted with a Dangerous Prayer.

Kim and I knew that we needed to be very selective in who we would share this news with in order to protect her from anyone who unknowingly would "speak death" over her or to her. We weren't looking for people who would just tell us what we wanted to hear but for those who would understand our position of faith that we were taking and be willing to support it. Our doctors were among our group. They were very direct with their medical advice and yet were very supportive in the fact that the final decision was not theirs. It was Kim's.

It didn't take very long to find out that there was a swarm of well-meaning people who have been affected by cancer. Mind-numbing fear has gripped so many that they felt they or their loved ones were completely at the mercy of a disease. Although Kim's father didn't have the same cancer as she, he still lost the battle to this sinister disease. So she had to constantly keep an eye on her own thoughts. She knew it would be problematic for someone who lost a loved one to cancer to understand how she and I were going to parade through this. That is the reason we decided to divvy out the details as they came with only those in our mastermind group. That way we knew we had others who were "standing in agreement" with us.

You may be asking, what does "standing in agreement" mean? The Bible says in Matthew 18:19, *"I also tell you this: If two of you agree here on earth concerning anything you ask, my Father in heaven will do it for you."* We actually believed this verse. We know that spiritual power is released and goes to work on the problem when more than one Christ follower mixes together their faith about a specific outcome.

Kim and I decided that we were going to mix our faith and speak life to her body and death to the cancer cells. We weren't brain-dead in denial and ignoring the diagnosis. We simply understood the power of spoken words. We heard the doctor's report but we made a galvanized decision to believe the life-giving words of our Lord. Kim knew she needed to dig into the Bible and find out what God had to say about sickness, disease and healing. Standing in agreement with her simply meant that whoever was praying for her would pray what we were praying. We realized that not everyone would understand or even be able to believe with us for her complete healing.

The first thing she knew she had to do was to load up her faith with overwhelming certainty. Romans 10:17 says, *"Faith comes by hearing and hearing by the Word of God."* She needed to elevate her faith level to line up with what the Bible had to say about her health, otherwise she would say one thing with her mouth but believe something different in her heart. The Bible says in James 1:8 that a double-minded man is unstable in all his ways and won't get answers to his prayers. She really wanted God to answer her Dangerous Prayer. She was desperate.

In fear and desperation, you may be reading this book right now. Kim's and my Dangerous Prayer for you as I am writing this is that through her story, God will give you dangerous faith to trust what He says through His Word. Keep in mind that a battle is a battle. Kim's battle was cancer, however yours may be that your finances have fallen down to your ankles and you are overexposed. It could be emotionally dead relationships in your marriage or with your children. You may be slowly losing to an undefeated addiction. How you win is the same. Be mean and pushy with your opposition. God will help you as long as you don't play fair. Always love people but pray dangerously. Go for it because what God did for Kim, He will do for you. He passionately loves you and you can trust Him!

Don't Miss the Supernatural Looking for the Spectacular.

Let's scrutinize Jesus' life while He walked on this earth to see if this is true. In Luke 5, He ran into a man with leprosy. The leper asked Jesus if He was willing to heal him. Jesus said, *"I will, you be clean."* Jesus obviously wanted to heal the leper. So He did. If Jesus were to bump into you, would he want to heal you? Yep! It's his nature to do that. Jesus is the same yesterday, today and forever, and He is no respecter of persons. If Jesus healed then, it is the will of God to be healed now. Sickness is flat-out not the will of God for anyone.

Luke 4:40 says, *"Now when the sun was setting, all they that had any sickness with divers diseases brought them unto him; and he laid his hands on every one of them, and healed them."* *Everybody* that came to Jesus was healed. Again, Jesus wanted to help *everyone.* In Matthew 4:23-25, we read, *"...and healing all manner of sickness and all manner of disease among the people..."* Jesus healed *all,* and all means, well...*all.* Also in Matthew 9:35-36 says, *"...and healing every sickness and every disease among them."*

The issue of *does God want people well or not* had to be answered in Kim's heart before she could really be healed. Otherwise she would have been going in two different directions at the same time. One, asking God to heal her and two, not really believing He could or would. I don't know about you, but I've never been able to go in more than one direction at a time.

Even when Kim lived her daily life trusting that she would be healed, her symptoms did not all go away immediately. I believe it was the Old Testament, King Hezekiah, who by faith was healed, but it was three days before he was able to get up and go up to the church. Jesus' promise is that "they shall recover". He doesn't say that it will always happen instantaneously. We stand on our faith, which is the confidence that what we are hoping will actually happen. *"Faith is the substance of things hoped for, the evidence of things not seen."* Hebrews 11:1

Deception, doubt and despair were all a flood of thoughts that Kim waded waist deep in just days before her surgery. In her weakest moments, the evil genius Satan began to bombard her thoughts with lies. *You may not make it. What would happen to your children if you don't come through this? After all, you are a stay-at-home mom and you homeschool your children. Don't you know those kids are totally dependent on you for everything? You know your husband can't work and take care of them, don't you?*

On the days she felt discouraged, frightened, and ready to give up, which maliciously visited her quite often, she repeatedly made the decision to stop those thoughts dead in their tracks and replace them with the thoughts of God's promises. She would open her mouth and speak the scriptures out loud so all could hear that she believed the words of the Lord providing healing for her inside and out. Doing this would cause her to feel strong and have courage.

One day after she had returned from a discouraging appointment with the surgeon, she needed fresh encouragement from the Lord. A true relationship relies on continued communication. God wants to be there for us every day. That means listening for Him to speak daily. He reminded Kim of a scripture she had shared with a friend of hers who had received a not so favorable report from a doctor a few months earlier. Isaiah 43:1-2. *"Fear not for I have redeemed you, I have called you by name, you are Mine. When you pass through the waters, I will be with you, and through the rivers, they will not overwhelm you. When you walk through the fire, you will not be burned or scorched, nor will the flame kindle upon you."* This scripture became a fresh word for Kim even though she had given it out to encourage a friend earlier. God was re-speaking it to her in a fresh way to meet the moment.

The Lord was tirelessly telling Kim that she belonged to Him and that He had His eye on her every step of the way. This was one of many times the Lord spoke to her heart. We read in the Old Testament how God spoke audibly. He speaks to us today as well. The Holy Spirit lives within each one of us the moment we ask Jesus into our hearts and become Christ-followers. When we pause and listen, He will speak to us every day. Our fresh encouragement comes from these times.

Not A Pretty Cry

Once when Kim was driving and about to get on the Interstate to pick up our kids from youth group, she felt a wave of fear come over her, and she began to cry. Not a pretty cry, either, but one of those ugly cries that you hope no one ever sees. She needed so desperately to hear from God. She didn't just want to read about this awesome God who wanted to heal her, she wanted this amazing God to speak to her on a personal level. She prayed dangerously and asked Him to speak to her directly. Sometimes we can all feel so far away from God.

As Kim merged onto the Interstate, she looked up and right there before her eyes was this amazing rainbow. She said, "Immediately the Lord spoke to my heart by reminding me of the scripture in II Corinthians 1:20 that says all of His promises are yes and Amen." Then a familiar praise song began to play in her mind over and over; reminding her to stay strong. She heard from God once again and faith filled her heart. She said, "At that moment, the fear left me and my weakness turned into God's strength in me!" No one is immune from being attacked by fear, but we don't have to be suffocated by it. We aren't powerless because we have a powerful friend—Jesus!

Kim didn't ignore the doctors' reports—that would not have been wise—but she didn't completely focus on them either. Her doctors' reports were based on facts, which were very important, however they were only part of the information needed to guide us. The bigger report was what God had promised not only in the Bible but what He had personally expressed to both Kim's and my heart. The doctor's report was based on facts, but God's word is based on truth, truth is greater than fact. Facts report a situation; truth transforms a situation. And it transformed Kim from the inside out. His truth not only built her faith and trust in Him but it made her a stronger person.

Catherine and Kim's Dangerous Prayer

A friend in our mastermind group, Catherine, had that calm, reassuring voice that brought peace to Kim. As Kim shared her deepest thoughts and emotions with Catherine, she would reassure Kim of the faithfulness of God. She would lovingly speak life, health and peace into the core of Kim's being. While writing this chapter with Kim four years later, as she thinks back to that time with tears streaming down her face, she still relives those precious moments. As her husband, I did my best to support Kim the entire time, but she also needed someone to nurture and lovingly help direct her like a spiritual mom, and that is exactly what Catherine did. Before Kim would hang up the phone, Catherine would always pray for her and share with her what she felt could be Kim's next step. Kim remembers calling her after her surgery and before they got off the phone, she asked Kim to pray dangerously with her.

"Thank you, Lord, for peace! By the blood of Christ, we cancel Satan's assignment against Kim's body, her marriage and her finances, in Jesus' name. She will let God and the Holy Spirit work in her life and body. You are our very powerful God. Kim receives your comfort and peace. She has the fruit of the Spirit in her life: love, joy, peace, patience, goodness, gentleness, meekness and self-control. She is bold as a lion, full of your courage and boldness. Her body is free of all cancer. Her immune system will arise to the occasion. Her body will heal itself. In the most powerful name of Jesus Christ."

A few months later Kim had her blood tested and it came back clean and clear of any cancer. Six months after that, which was one year after she began treatment with Dr. Don Colbert, her PET scan was clear of all cancer as well. And today, Kim's annual blood work repeatedly comes back with no trace of cancer. Praise God!

We were somehow able to see the end from the beginning. God's loving help and godly friends made all the difference when it came to dealing with fear and the disease that had viciously attacked my wife's body. We held on to God's promises and our friends with all the faith, courage and tears we could muster, and it worked. Not because we were magically directing our destiny, but because we trusted someone much bigger than us, who from His perspective, could see it finished and in our favor. And we trusted Him with that. Our best interest is always His first interest.

Be Dangerous

You see, we are no more special than you. If you just got "the news," then stop what you are doing right now—yes, in the middle of all the fear and emotions screaming in your ears—and pray. Don't pray a nice little Sunday school prayer. Pray a Dangerous Prayer like we prayed. It doesn't mean you will instantly have all the answers, but by God it will put fear on notice that you will not give in to its trickery, and you will not lay down and just let this—whatever this is—win. By God, be dangerous and dismantle your fear with God's love through his Word (the Bible), godly friends, worship and your Dangerous Prayers!

CLOSING RANTS
Where Do You Go From Here?

If you have read this far...you're ready. So get out there, violently take the Kingdom by force.

You have a Dangerous Prayer, you just may not know it yet. Even if you have never thought of it, your Dangerous Prayer is in your heart. And it is not just you telling God what you want. It's about trusting that He loves you in the hard times and in the good times. He will let you know when it's time to say back to Him what he has already in His heart to bless you. Yes, it requires faith. Yes, it requires a little boldness in the face of barrenness, but what you see now is not everything there is to be seen.

Christ-followers live in two worlds, the seen and the unseen. Since nothing happens until we pray, prayer is the first thing that should happen. It does take a while to get used to a life of praying first, then doing. Prayer is following God's heart and wanting more of His life to be our life. I know you might be saying, "What the heck does that mean?" Just spend more time with the "noise" of your life shut down. It may cost you time from your fun stuff, but do it. The more you do it, the better you will be at hearing God and praying what He puts in your heart. Don't worry your little head about getting it right the first time.

Just do it.

Even if you are wrong the first time you pray dangerously, God won't let you be wrong for long. So what do you have just sloshing around in your heart that needs to pour out your tongue to God? Come on; go for it. Write it down and speak it into the universe where you, the angels, God and yes, even the devil can hear it. Don't be afraid of what God thinks about it. Odds are the more outrageous it is, the more likely God put it in there.

Think about it. Why would the enemy of your very existence, Satan, put something outrageously good for you and the kingdom of God in your heart to pray?

Wait for it...wait for it... He wouldn't! Yes, you are very welcome! I just cleared it up for you. No, Satan wants you broke, sick or better yet for him, dead. In the gospel of John we read the words of Jesus himself and whatever you remember, please let it be this:

"The enemy (Satan) comes to kill, steal and destroy, but I have come to give you life and that more abundantly." John 10:10 KJV

Don't mix up who wants you dead and Who wants you to live abundantly. If you get a wild hair of an idea to believe or speak any shade of death over your life or someone else's, that's bad. And it did not come from God. It came from the other guy, the one who hates you. Yes, he can give you thoughts too. I know you might not like to hear that, but it's true. Now he cannot control you if you are a Christ follower, but he can give you some nasty stuff to think about.

So if the stuff you are thinking is NOT good, replace it with the GOOD STUFF. Like the Snapple commercials say, fill your mind with the good stuff and hang around Christ-followers who speak life, not death. Listen to life-giving pastors and get crazy and fanatical and maybe even read the Bible a little every day. You don't stop thinking bad thoughts. You REPLACE them with the good stuff.

Over time you will start praying the good stuff back to your heavenly Father. And good stuff will begin to happen to you. I know you've probably heard, "Good things happen to good people." Wrong! Good things happen to those who believe good things happen to them. And you can quote me on that.

This principle will happen even to people who are on the fringe like my friend, crazy Henry. He's not really crazy. He just has that one eye that won't look straight at me when we talk. Kind of freaks me out a bit.

"Guard your heart above all else, for it determines the course of your life." Proverbs 4:23 NLT

Words are Things

Words held in your heart over time will eventually wrap themselves in reality. In other words, what you think about, especially if it is mixed with emotions, will eventually actually happen in your life. I know it sounds a little spooky, but it's true. So it's very important to "guard" your heart, or more specifically, your thoughts.

This principle, "words are things and will eventually clothe themselves in their physical likeness" is nothing new.

Hebrews 11:1 states that, *"Faith is the SUBSTANCE of things hoped for and the evidence of things unseen."* (Emphasis added) Faith is what you see in your heart. It's a combination of what you imagine and feel is true. This combination creates prayers that get released into the air.

God only wants to answer the good stuff but your enemy will try also to answer the bad stuff. So don't be afraid. Just be on purpose with your thoughts and ideas. Especially those emotionally charged ones.

Here's an important but little-known secret about prayer. *You pray all the time.* Yes, folks, you heard it here first, you pray constantly. What is in your heart goes up to God. The good stuff He loves to answer but the junk—and we all have some—He cannot answer. Why do you say that? 'Cause He is crazy in love with us and will try to talk us out of the "the junk." How does He do it? Through reading the Bible and stuff like that.

Anyway, we do and we have and we live and we pray what is in our hearts. There. I'm out of breath, but I said it.

"...For the Lord sees not as man sees: man looks on the outward appearance, but the Lord looks on the heart." 1 Samuel 16:7 ESV

So prayer is as much what you hold in your heart as what you say with your mouth. What does that look like? And how can you be aware of what is in your heart?

Example time. Right now while I'm writing this, I'm thinking about some knuckleheads I know who get on my nerves. Hey, don't judge. Yes, pastors are human too, and we have to decide what to do with those thoughts just like you. I can just let these thoughts ride and get more ticked off and think, "Get 'em, God." He just isn't in the business of dishing out holy lightning bolts upon my command. The way to re-direct my heart prayers is to replace my thoughts with what God really thinks.

"But I say to you, love your enemies and bless the one who curses you, and do what is beautiful to the one who

hates you and pray over those who take you by force and persecute you." Matthew 5:44 Aramaic Bible in Plain English.

So there you go. God just told me what to hold in my heart and how to respond to the knuckleheads in my life. He did not say I had to like what they do but how to deal with it.

The more you hold the good stuff in your heart, the more you think like God, so the more you pray God's will.

So Let's Wrap It Up Here.

You have at least one Dangerous Prayer rolling around in your heart, so get it out so the universe can take a good look at it. Don't be shy.

Watch what you let bounce around in your noggin, 'cause that stuff gets stuck in your heart and becomes a part of you. As I like to say, "Think about what you *think about*." A journal or an honest friend can help with this; one's just louder than the other.

Replace the bad thoughts with the good stuff. Be patient with yourself. It takes a while, but it will happen. You'll be praying God's will out loud before you know it.

That's it. Now, go get 'em, tiger!

To your spiritual health,

Alex E. Anderson

P.S. As I was finishing up this book it occurred to me how many little practical things that happened in each one of my friends' lives that were important to their success in praying Dangerous Prayers that could not be included in this book without it becoming, oh, I don't know, at least 900 pages or so. And who wants to read 900 pages? When I see those size books, I think, "Man! I don't want to wade through all those words just to get the 'nuggets' that I'm really looking for and need right now.

P.P.S. I also realized that you may be like me; I'd rather watch someone do what I want to do and have them give me a little bit of instruction, then let me try it versus, again, wading through 900 pages of words. So I'm creating a video series for the "stuff" that I could not stuff into this book, or into you, for that matter. Be sure you are on my email list by signing up at www.dangerous-prayers.com and I will let you know when it is available. I will give you a sampling of it to see if you like it. There will be hours of short video segments of little but powerful and actually life-changing habits that you can instantly practice in your prayer life. God is so cool. He doesn't wait until we are perfect Christ-followers to jump right in and help out.

Oh yeah! I almost forgot, for the note takers like me, I wrote a short workbook to go along with the videos.

Hope it helps!

AKNOWLEDGEMENTS

You guys are awesome!

Here are the great folks who helped me pull this off:

The men of my "Lightbulbs" small group...this is all your fault.

My brother, Shane Anderson, who said, "So when are you going to write a book?" and I said, "Book? What book?"

Pastor Randy Bezet for creating the most life-giving church in America.

Kelly Stilwell, primary editor and the biggest "poke-n-the-ribs" I needed to keep going and finish. Thank you, my friend!

Stephanie Ferber, for her tireless hours and hours of cleaning up my wandering words.

Mike Tullio for his edits and kicking awesome title, *Dangerous Prayers*.

Roger Conley for looking over my shoulder.

My friends who allowed me the privilege of using their real life stories.

Kayla Danielle Photography, for my killer book cover.

Kayla, Evan and Victoria, my children, for doing without Dad while he was in his study taking a nap...I mean writing.

And to Amy Greene, whose final edits and comments took this book to a whole other level.

Most of all my best friend and wife, Kim. She has been my inspiration so many times when I had none.

My other best friend, Holy Spirit, for the confidence to write something He would use to help others.

ABOUT THE AUTHOR

Alex Anderson serves as a strategist and a Senior Associate Pastor at Bayside Community Church in Bradenton/Sarasota, Florida, a church named by Outreach Magazine in 2011 as the 10th Fastest Growing Church in America. He is the Vice President of Relate Coaching, a ministry that specializes in relational church growth. He also writes the monthly Spiritual Wellness Column for the South West Florida's Health and Wellness Magazine.

Alex has been married for over twenty-seven years to the same woman—his best friend, Kim Anderson, and together they eventually raised three life-giving young adults. He has been a minister for over thirty years, but don't hold that against him. He was also a businessman for eighteen of those years.

You may contact Alex by email at:
alex.anderson@alexanderson.org